Land of the
Loyalists

Their struggle to shape the Maritimes

Ronald Rees

NIMBUS
PUBLISHING LTD

Nimbus Publishing Limited
PO Box 9301, Station A
Halifax, NS   B3K 5N5
(902)455-4286

Design: Arthur Carter
Cover image: Joseph Brown Comingo (1784-1821),
    View of Saint John, New Brunswick, 1814,
    watercolour over graphite on wove paper,
    New Brunswick Museum, Saint John, N.B.

Printed and bound in Canada

Canadian Cataloguing in Publication Data
Rees, Ronald, 1935–
    The loyalist imprint
    Includes bibliographical references.

ISBN 1-55109-274-3
    1. United Empire loyalists -- New Brunswick. 2.
Architecture -- New Brunswick -- History. 3.
Landscape gardening -- New Brunswick -- History. 4.
New Brunswick -- Civilization. I. Title.

FC2471.3.R43 2000   971.5
F1043.R43 2000

Canadä

Nimbus Publishing acknowledges financial support for our
publishing activities from the Government of Canada through
the Book Publishing Industry Development Program (BPIDP),
and the Canada Council.

Although, for this book,
Nimbus followed several
official federal and provincial
sources listing the "Saint
John River," the standard
local spelling is "St. John
River"; we apologize, in
advance, for any confusion.

Contents

Dedication

To Diana

British forces leaving New York.

National Archives of Canada

The Loyalist Blueprint

F or most migrants a new land is an intimidating question mark. Unfamiliar with the terrain, the customs and—very often—the language, the typical newcomer is a study in passivity, a cipher awaiting directions from the powerful or the knowledgeable. Not so the Loyalists who came to New Brunswick and Nova Scotia after the War of the American Revolution (1776-1782). Although not the cultivated, Harvard-educated aristocrats of a once-popular mythology, they were far from standard migrants or refugees. Most were American-born, all had some experience of North American conditions, and most of the leaders were, in fact, well-placed and well-educated. The distinction did not escape the Loyalist promoters and spokesmen. "There are assembled here," wrote their most devoted chronicler, Edward Winslow, "an immense multitude, not of dissolute vagrants such as commonly make the first efforts to settle new countries, but gentlemen of education, farmers formerly independent, and reputable mechanics, who by the fortune of war have been deprived of their property." Sir Guy Carleton, Commander-in-Chief of the British forces in North America, relayed an almost identical message when introducing the first wave of Loyalists to the Governor of Nova Scotia: "These persons are to be considered as real efficient settlers, already acquainted with all the necessary arts of culture and habituated to settlements of the like kind: and who, independent of their just claims, will bring a large accession of strength as well as of population into the province."

Although uprooted and debilitated by a long and, for them, unsuccessful war, they came with expectations or, as we might say now, with attitude. Far from being ciphers ready to do the bidding of colonial officials, the Loyalists arrived in Nova Scotia—of which New Brunswick was then a part—with a blueprint of the world they intended to inhabit. The rough and heavily treed land might have given them pause but the leaders were in no doubt as to the kind of political and social patterns they intended to impose upon it. People who, as one Digby Loyalist remarked, "had quit the lands of [their] nativity" rather than live under "the Tyrannic power of a republican Government" were

Sir Guy Carleton.

not about to revert to anarchy. The Loyalist objective in Nova Scotia, as several of their spokesmen were at pains to point out, was to create a world so well-ordered that it would arouse jealousy in the still-fomenting American colonies. "I entertain the most sanguine hope," wrote Sir Guy Carleton, "that the provinces which are to remain under His Majesty's dominion will suddenly become powerful, and objects of envy to those whom in the present moment, madly renounce the most equitable and wise system of government, for anarchy and distraction." The outlines of that enviable new world had been clearly drawn in the plans for "New Ireland," a never-realized province between rebellious New England and loyal New Scotland, now Nova Scotia.

The architects of New Ireland were a small group of Loyalists and British government officials led by William Knox, an under-secretary of state in the American Department in London and an implacable opponent of republicanism. By bringing under British control the territory between the Penobscot and the St Croix Rivers, Knox hoped to provide a home for Loyalist refugees then crowding into British strongholds such as New York, Boston, and Philadelphia. By publicizing the plan he also hoped to reassure Loyalist troops that they would be guaranteed a haven whatever the outcome of the war. The New Ireland plan called for the seizure of the mouth of the Penobscot and the establishment of a civil authority made up of "meritorious" Loyalists. The prospective governor was the London-exiled Thomas Hutchinson who, as Chief Justice, Lieutenant Governor, and finally Royal Governor of Massachusetts, had been one of the most unbending of the "Tory" office holders. "It has been his principle from a boy," Samuel Adams noted coldly, "that mankind are to be governed by the discerning few." Even so, Hutchinson, who is said to have been dismissive of plans and ideas that displeased him, had no desire to govern New Ireland. After a briefing from Knox, he confided to his diary that he thought the measure "most preposterous" and resolved to convey these sentiments to Knox in as prudent a manner as possible.

But Hutchinson's reservations changed nothing. In June 1779 the British sent from Halifax a six hundred-strong expeditionary force to occupy the mouth of the Penobscot and build a fort. Attacked by a land and sea expedition from Massachusetts, the force was saved only by the timely intervention of the British fleet. But neither the victory nor the building of Fort George could generate widespread enthusiasm for the New Ireland scheme. Hutchinson continued to regard it balefully while Admiral Collier, the commander of the British fleet, dismissed the country he had been at some pains to secure as "a wilderness fit only for beasts." Nor were ordinary Loyalists, who expected a British victory in the war, drawn to New Ireland. The chief exceptions were merchant families from Falmouth (now Portland) attracted by a coastal fort expected to become the capital of a new province. To urge official recognition of the province, in May 1780 they sent a spokesman—their surgeon and chaplain Dr John Caleff—to London. There he spoke of a people "destitute of Law and Gospel" whose distress could be relieved only by the attentions of a minister of the Church of England and the creation of a government separate from Massachusetts Bay.

King George III of Great Britain.

Private Collection

In London both William Knox and Lord George Germain, the Secretary of State for American affairs, were primed to act. Taking Knox's previously prepared plan for a model Loyalist colony they produced, between the 7–9 of August, 1780, a constitution expressly designed to counter "the prevailing disposition of the people to Republicanism." It gave absolute power to the British Parliament. There was to be a governor (Peter Oliver of Massachusetts rather than the reluctant Thomas Hutchinson) and a privy council supported by an upper house or legislature appointed by the Crown. Provided the appointees gave no cause for removal, royal appointments were for life. As a brake on democratic or republican sentiments, there was to be no elected assembly until circumstances required one and even then its control of finances would be limited. Prominent Loyalists would always be directed to the higher, appointed councils and spared the indignity—inescapable in the rebellious colonies—of submitting to the vote. As in the old world, land would confer status. Large tracts were to be granted to the most deserving Loyalists, who would preside over tenant farmers and labourers. Although their loyalty had been based on resistance to Revolutionary landlords, Knox pointed out that the tenantry of Hudson Valley estates had been exceptionally supportive of the Crown. In New Ireland, the *quid pro quo* for acquiring land, whether by purchase, inheritance, or grant, would be a declara-

The British Army evacuates Boston—Loyalist refugees depart for Nova Scotia.

National Archives of Canada

tion of allegiance to the King. Laws, designed by the Attorney General's office in London, would, of course, be English.

To close the colonial net, Knox and Germain proposed that the Church of England be the only recognized church and that the country be divided into parishes, not townships, each with a glebe land—the portion of land routinely assigned to a member of the clergy. In the older colonies, Anglicans were usually, and often fervently, loyal. To seal the marriage of church and state, the constitution for New Ireland also required that the governor be the highest judge in the ecclesiastical court and the filler of all benefices. Powers of ordination were to be vested in a vicar-general, the way being thus opened for a bishop. Ministers' stipends were to be guaranteed by the government. According to the

Reverend William Walter, former rector of Trinity Church, Boston, the object of the Knox/Germain document was, once again, to incite envy—by its "liberality" to show the American provinces "the great advantages of being a portion of the Empire and living under the protection of the British government."

The Knox/Germain plan for New Ireland clearly pleased both the cabinet and the king, the former approving it on August 10, 1780, and the latter, with only a few minor corrections, on the following day. But despite government and royal support the plan was never realized. Succumbing to a fit of legal scruple—induced, according to Knox, by pique at not being made a peer—the Attorney General, Alexander Wedderburn, witheld his consent on grounds that the lands between the Penobscot and the St. Croix, once having been granted to the Massachusetts Bay Colony, still belonged to it. The British government could not, he insisted, cre-

The British surrender at Yorktown, 1781.

Private collection

ate a new colony within the boundaries of an already established one. Massachusetts might have been in open rebellion with Great Britain but the ratification of New Ireland, according to Wedderburn, would still have constituted a violation of its charter rights.

In deference to Wedderburn, no action was taken, but within a year arcane principle had been overtaken by events. The surrender of the English commander Lord Cornwallis at Yorktown in October 1781, and the fall of Lord North's Tory ministry in 1782, put an end to the plans of Germain and Knox and dashed the hopes of Loyalists everywhere. Caleff continued to urge the implementation of the plan, arguing that the Penobscot could be a base for the recapture of the New England colonies, but the scheme was, as Lord North informed him, impossible. The incoming Whig government was pledged to a policy of conciliation with the United States, and John Adams of Massachusetts, the most intractable of the American negotiators at the Treaty of Paris, was in no mood to make territorial concessions to people whom his countrymen regarded as "Dishonours and Destroyers." Adams was also determined to root out, as one writer described it, "the viperine nest at Penobscot."

At Versailles (where the Treaty was signed on 30 November, 1782) Great Britain, to the dismay of the Loyalists, agreed outright to the independence of the thirteen states. In exchange for Maine, the British negotiators exacted a promise that Congress would "earnestly recommend" to the individual states, over which it had no powers of compulsion, that the rights and property of non-combatants be restored and that combatants be given a year to leave the country. But without the authority of law no recommendation, however earnest, could have prevented retaliation. Whereas the British had been merely the enemy, their active American supporters—even though they had not taken the oath of allegiance to the republic—were near-traitors. Faced with the wrath of angry and vengeance-seeking Patriots, between eighty and one hundred thousand of them (roughly one fifth of the total number of Loyalists) began making plans to leave their country.

Loyalists landing at the site of present-day Saint John, 1783. A romanticised view but it does suggest a setting rugged enough to have reduced some refugees to tears. (John David Kelly)

Chapter One

The New Land

For Loyalists who had taken up arms during the revolution, or been active in other ways, flight was the only option. The wealthy, the well-connected, and the exceptionally ambitious were partial to Great Britain. Slave-owning southerners, on the other hand, favoured the Bahamas and the British West Indies despite the threat, in the latter islands, of excessive heat and yellow fever. But for most northern and southern Loyalists the only practical havens were the remaining provinces of British North America. Prince Edward Island, then owned almost entirely by absentee proprietors, was effectively closed to land-seeking settlers but the vast countryside of Ontario, Quebec, and Nova Scotia attracted an estimated sixty thousand men, women, and children. Among them were approximately 5,000 Blacks (both free Blacks and "servants for life") and an equal number of disbanded regular British and German troops.

Reports on Nova Scotia, which was to get the lion's share of the north-bound refugees, were encouraging. It was only a short sea voyage from New York and, edging into the Atlantic, it was closer to Britain than any of the American states, as well as being a convenient springboard for markets in the West Indies. Its harbours might thicken with ice but they were never quite blocked so settlers could be supplied easily by water. Forests, fish, and game were plentiful and the winters, though cold, were said to be bearable. For New Englanders, too, Nova Scotia to some extent was home away from home: climate and terrain were both familiar and for more than a century and a half, New England farmers and fishermen had been settling on the Atlantic and the Fundy coasts.

Yet most Loyalists contemplating flight or awaiting embarkation in the British-held ports were apprehensive. They were unconvinced by the reports and loath to entrust themselves, as one of them remarked, to the "deserts of Nova

Scotia." Nor was the Patriot press taken in by the encomiums of the Loyalist scouts and agents. A rough land rumoured to be snowbound for six months of the year and fog-bound for much of the rest quickly became "Nova Scarcity." Not even the usually magnanimous George Washington could resist a parting shot when taking his leave of the departing Tories: "Gentlemen, I wish you all well. I wish you all may go to Heaven, but you must go there by way of Nova Scotia."

The Patriot view that Great Britain had been left with the rump of North America was shared by William Cobbett, the crusading English writer and pamphleteer who as a sergeant-major in the British regular army spent six years (1785-91) in the Maritimes. Although impressed by the rich soils and natural meadows of the river bottomlands—in a garden at Fredericton he grew "as fine cabbages, turnips, and garden things of the hardy sorts, as any man need wish to see"—he had no illusions about the agricultural potential of the region as a whole. If North America were an ox then New Brunswick and Nova Scotia represented "the horns, the head, the neck, the shins, and the hoof." The choice parts—"the ribs, the sirloin, [and] the kidneys"—belonged to the United States. In a more literal mood, he described Nova Scotia and New Brunswick as "one great heap of rocks, covered with fir trees, with here and there a little strip of land capable of cultivation." Dependent on the United States for meat, flour, fruits, and even cabbages, and blanketed in snow for seven months of the year, the provinces were, in short, "the most barren, the most villainous piece of waste land." Compared with the "fat" meadows and gardens of Kent, or the lush valleys of the United States, the soils of the provinces were as "the thin shell upon the top of a gravel pit."

Those Loyalists who found themselves in the bleakest parts of the Maritimes were just as disparaging: "The most inhospitable [land] ... that ever mortal set foot on," wrote one. "The winter is of insupportable length and coldness, only a few spots fit to cultivate, and the land is covered with a cold, spongy moss, instead of grass, and the entire country is wrapt in the gloom of perpetual fog." Southerners who had come, in Nova Scotia's Governor Parr's phrase, from the "burning sands" of the Carolinas and East Florida to "the frozen coasts of Nova Scotia," were particularly aggrieved. Shocked by the roughness of the land and "much frightened" by the weather, many asked if they could not be re-settled in a place where the climate, for southern constitutions, was less "inhospitable and severe." Even southern slaves objected to being removed to Nova Scotia, one aggressively enough that her owner, from East Florida, was forced to sell her "at a great loss" because of "her aversion to go to [Nova Scotia], Halifax being a very cold climate."

Even allowing for hyperbole and an eighteenth century distaste for rough country, nature had been far from generous in the Maritimes. Winters, though not as frightening as many of the Loyalists had imagined, were cold and long and large parts of the region, which is simply the northern end of the Appalachians, were uncultivable and unprepossessing. Ice sheets had scraped clean the high ground and roughed up the low so that, except in some of the valleys, soils were thin, stony, and acid. And for a region midway between the equator and the poles, the growing season was remarkably cool and short.

Politically, too, Nova Scotia was suspect. Scattered throughout the region were New England settlers (Planters) who, though ostensibly neutral during the war, were suspected of duplicity—of having "loyalty upon the tip of their tongues" and "rebellion in their hearts." There were also doubts about the competence of the governor, Colonel John Parr, and the intentions of his Halifax advisers. The roughly 15,000 inhabitants of peninsular Nova Scotia were far from pleased at the prospect of being outnumbered by Loyalists and they made little effort to disguise their displeasure. Edward Winslow dismissed their leaders as a "nest of pickaroons" whom he accused of wanting to deposit the Loyalists in the poorest and most barren parts of the peninsula. To realize the dream of New Ireland, the Loyalists clearly needed a fresh start in a place of their own—a *tabula rasa*.

The idea of dividing Nova Scotia into two provinces along the Bay of Fundy was first aired officially by Edward Winslow in July 1783 during a reconnaissance of the Saint John Valley. As muster master general for the Loyalist forces, Winslow had been charged with finding havens for the disbanded regiments. For Loyalists on the north side of the Bay, government from Halifax was both cumbersome and inhibiting. Communications were slow, and whereas Halifax preferred coastal settlement—for purposes of accessibility and control—most of the Loyalists had eyes only for the fertile and richly-forested middle reaches of the valley. It was rumoured, too, that Governor Parr would soon dissolve Nova Scotia's Long Parliament (which had been sitting since 1770) and call elections before the Loyalists were eligible to vote. For the Saint John contingent, government at a distance by people with republican tendencies was hardly appealing.

Once aired, the idea of separate provinces on each side of the Bay proved uncontainable. The prospect of a new Loyalist province revived hopes dashed by the collapse of the plan for New Ireland and it promised to double the number of offices available to the Loyalist hopefuls lining the corridors of the Colonial Office in London. Petitions for the division fell into receptive hands and in June 1784 partition duly followed. London's official position on the division was that communications between Halifax and the "the back settlements" were insupportably difficult and slow, but for William Knox in London and the Loyalists in Saint John the greater reason was the heady prospect of a fresh start. Edward Winslow thought the new province should aim at nothing less than a government that would be "the most Gentlemanlike one on earth" and a society that would be—what else?—"the envy of the American States."

The "Old Inhabitants"

Cobbett may have exaggerated the limitations of Nova Scotia and New Brunswick as places for European settlement but neither province was a gift to colonists. Both were rich in timber and their coastal waters teemed with fish, but many questioned whether they were capable of sustaining a large farming population. Cobbett's "few strips of cultivable land" might have been an uncompromising assessment of the farming prospects but it was not an inaccurate one. From a Loyalist point of view, too, the amount of land available for farming was restricted by previous settlement and by land grants. Loyalists managed to work their way into most of the settled parts of Nova Scotia but, in effect, they had to make do with the left-overs. Earlier colonists had taken up the more arable and accessible land and much of the good land that remained was held by promoters, speculators, and office-holders.

To replace the Acadians deported or driven into the wilderness on the eve of the Seven Years' War, Governor Lawrence of Nova Scotia appealed directly to New Englanders. Great Britain's objective was to replace French-speaking Roman Catholics with English-speaking Protestants and, at the same time, discourage land-hungry New England farmers from spilling westward across the Appalachians into Indian territories. In a January 1759 proclamation Governor Lawrence offered groups of settlers 100,000-acre townships of "the best and most profitable land." As Congregationalists, the New Englanders were also promised exemption from all the rates and taxes designated for the Church of England. So attractive was the offer that between seven and eight thousand from Connecticut, Rhode Island, and Eastern Massachusetts moved into Nova Scotia: farmers into the Annapolis Valley, Chignecto, and the Minas Basin and fishermen and traders, mostly from Nantucket and Cape Cod, into harbours and inlets on the Atlantic and Fundy Coasts. A handful of fishermen and traders made for Passamaquoddy Bay and the mouth of the Saint John River but most settled for the choice harbours and inlets on the southwestern coast of the Nova Scotia peninsula.

To promote settlement in what was still a cavernously empty region the colonial government, in exchange for promises to attract settlers, also granted large blocks of land to individuals; in one convulsive episode in 1765 almost three million acres (one-and-a-half million in Nova Scotia and more than one million in what is now New Brunswick) were handed over in seventeen days. Ulimately, through a failure to improve the grants or pay the annual property rents, much of this land would be re-possessed or "escheated" but in 1782, on the eve of the Loyalist migration, almost all of the colony's useful land had passed from Crown ownership into private hands. In peninsular Nova Scotia, all that remained for the Loyalists were parts of Digby and Annapolis counties and rough coastal tracts along the Northumberland Strait and in Shelburne, Halifax, and Guysborough counties. Any one of these coastal regions might have been the crucible for that quintessential Maritime expression, "you can't live on a view."

With a population of up to a 1,000 Mi'kmaq and Maliseet Indians and about 2,500 Acadians and New Englanders, New Brunswick in 1782–83 was still a wilderness. As farmers and traders the Europeans were concentrated in the Saint John Valley, the Passamaquoddy region at the mouth of the St Croix, and the salt marshes at the head of the Bay of Fundy. Between the Saint John and the St Croix Rivers lay sixty miles of uninhabited and, as one observer saw it, uninhabitable country. As in peninsular Nova Scotia, much of the good land had already been granted. In the Saint John Valley most of the river land below

Islands and intervals in the Saint John Valley below Fredericton, late nineteenth century.

George Thomas Taylor, Public Archives of New Brunswick.

Fredericton was in the hands of the Saint John River Society, a consortium of army officers who had served in the French and Indian wars. As a reward for service, and on the strength of a promise to colonize the region, in 1765 they were granted five townships—roughly 400,000 acres—in the lower valley and an island in Passamaquoddy Bay. The most successful settlement was at Maugerville, founded in 1763 by a group of farmers from Essex County, Massachusetts, who divided the township into lots and built a Congregational Church. By 1783 the township had a population of about 500.

Uplands and bottomlands at Kingsclear in the Saint John Valley above Fredericton, late nineteenth century.

For both the Acadians, who had settled in the middle reaches of the valley, and the New England Planters, the approach of the Loyalists was unsettling. Afraid of losing their religion and culture, and unwilling to tolerate neighbours notorious, as one of them put it, for their "many dissipations" (dancing, card-playing, and a love of finery seem to have been the most serious), the Acadians moved far upstream to the district of Madawaska. In the middle and lower valley, this left only the Mi'kmaq and Maliseet Indians and the thousand or so Planters in Maugerville and the neighbouring townships. Under the spell of the evangelist Henry Alline, who made at least three visits to Maugerville, the Planters also feared contamination by the Loyalists: wantons of the "utmost dissipation." But having settled on fabulously rich bottom or "interval" land they were not about to let "grief and discontent" precipitate a move from a place where providence had clearly smiled on them. Three years after the settlement, Beamsley Glasier described their river lands: "flat, not a stone or pebble. It runs level...such land as I cannot describe. The New England people have never ploughed but harrowed in their grain."

Of least trouble to the land-seeking Loyalists were the earliest of all the inhabitants: the Mi'kmaq and the Maliseets.

As small, weak bands and former allies of the French they were not deemed worthy of courtship, far less concessions. The Loyalists coveted the river frontages of the Saint John from which the Indians fished, and the intervals on which they grew corn, so the Indians were compelled, as Edward Winslow remarked nonchalantly, "to leave the banks of the rivers...and hunt on other grounds."

The Ideal Landscape

For the Loyalist leaders and planners, the landscape never far from the mind's eye was English pastorale, that soothing assemblage of hedged fields, farm and manor houses, which was as much a social, political, and aesthetic entity as an economic one. In England, as in Augustan Rome, a well-ordered land was regarded as a prerequisite of the well-governed state. Throughout the English lowlands, large estates, subdivided into tenant farms and presided over by manor houses set in landscaped grounds, dominated the countryside. For the rich, the ideal arrangement was a house—and government position—in town, and a property in the country.

Patrician sentiments surfaced early. In New York in July 1783 fifty-five prominent Loyalists, known subsequently as the Committee of Fifty-five, requested land grants of 5,000 acres each. The usual civilian portion was no more than a few hundred acres. The land, which was to be chosen by the committee's agents, would be free of quitrent—a convention whereby land was held in exchange for loyalty and military services—surveyed at government expense, and deeded promptly to the grantees. In part, the grants were to compensate for wartime losses of property and position but the larger motivation, so the petitioners claimed, was high-minded. A landlord-tenant arrangement, with the landowners providing roads, mills, livestock and, above all, guidance for their tenants would, they contended, encourage deference in the lower orders and strengthen the authority of the Crown. As a spokesman put it, "the Fifty-five [were] humbly of the opinion that the settling of such a number of Loyalists, of the most respectable characters, who have constantly had great influence in his Majesty's American dominions, will be highly advantageous in diffusing and supporting a spirit of attachment to the British constitution, as well as to His Majesty's royal person and family." In effect, they were proposing a return to the proprietary system of colonization used in the seventeenth century.

Although the Fifty-five's request greatly exceeded the standard civilian allotment, the petitioners saw no reason to be defensive. Allotments of five thousand acres would do no more than put them on the same footing as British field officers at the end of the Seven Years' War in 1763. They were also smaller than many of the grants in the Hudson Valley and the former Middle Colonies and only one quarter the size of holdings on the island of St. John, now Prince Edward Island.

Banner of the Nova Scotia Loyalists.

Public Archives of Canada

In 1767 most of the Island had been granted by lottery to 64 London proprietors on the understanding that they would both develop and settle it. To retain title to their 20,000-acre grants, the proprietors were required to pay a substantial quitrent and improve and populate their properties with North American settlers or Protestant settlers from overseas. Although not specified in the grants, it seems to have been generally understood that the settlers' lots would be rented and, as a corollary of this, that the Island would have a ruling class of gentlemen landowners and a working class of tenant farmers. On the understanding that the proprietors, from the income from their estates, would bear the entire costs of administration, the Island, in 1769, was granted a separate government. By 1775, however, the proprietors had managed to attract only fifteen hundred settlers, recruited mostly in Ireland, Scotland, and England, to long leaseholds on landed estates. More than forty of the estates were still empty but, the Island being a separate fiefdom, these were not easily recoverable by escheat. Quitrents fell badly off and when the American Revolution brought immigration to a halt the Crown reluctantly assumed the costs of government.

From New York, Sir Guy Carleton forwarded the Fifty-five's petition to Governor Parr in Halifax. Sir Guy did not recommend the scheme but by vouching for the four agents sent to Nova Scotia he clearly approved of it. Most of the good land in Nova Scotia might already have been granted but the province was still very thinly settled and the Commander-in-Chief, like others of his class, would have subscribed to the principle that in the colonies aristocracy was the most effective instrument for preserving the authority of the Crown. But whatever the merits of the scheme, the Loyalist rank and file were in no mood to tolerate patrician sentiments. No sooner had the Fifty-five's petition been made public than, following a protest meeting in a New York tavern, they drafted one of their own. It charged that granting the "most fertile spots and desirable situations" in Nova Scotia would present them with a Hobson's choice: either settle for the leftovers, the "barren or remote Lands," or submit to being tenants of landlords whom they considered superior in nothing but "deeper Art and keener Policy." Any distinction that fell to these, they contended, came more from "the repeated favours of Government than by either the greatness of their sufferings, or the importance of their services."

Silhouette of Nova Scotia Governor John Parr.

Startled by the vehement tone of the petition, to which there were 600 signatories, Sir Guy Carleton withdrew his support for the scheme but not before a surveyor, under warrant from Governor Parr, had set out for Annapolis and St. Mary's Bay. The Fifty-five's agents had settled tentatively for lands on each side of the Sissiboo River, but if these proved to be insufficient or unsuitable they reserved the right to choose lots from any of the vacant lands in the province. Surveying began but in response to Sir Guy Carleton's retraction, Governor Parr reduced the size of the grants from five to one thousand acres and then offered them only to petitioners who were actually in Nova Scotia. The disgruntled agents appealed to the Colonial Office, but government officials were no longer in a mood to entertain dreams of a society governed by gentlemen farmers. They ruled that in the absence of tenants, which the Loyalist rank and file had no intention of becoming, large land grants would make speculators or absentee owners of even the most well-meaning landowners.

The Survey and Land Distribution

To discourage speculation and the hoarding and locking up of land, the British government's land policy in Nova Scotia and New Brunswick was restrained and, for the period, even-handed. Subsequent redistribution changed the dimensions of many of the lots but the initial grants were relatively small. Civilians of standing, "such as have suffered most," received grants of 1,000 acres but for all other civilians, or refugees, the official allowance was 100 acres for each head of family and 50 acres for each additional member. All were exempt from the payment of fees, quitrents, and other monetary obligations and all grantees were

The camp of a surveying party near Stanley, New Brunswick (Philip Harry, 1833).

National Archives of Canada

eligible to apply for additional land provided they had fulfilled the terms of their first grant or could pay the quitrent on the land being applied for. Only military grants were graded. Privates were allowed 100 acres, non-commissioned officers 200, subalterns 500, captains 700, and field-officers 1,000. Groups of military or civilian settlers who wished to live together could also apply for a block grant. In addition to land, Loyalists were supplied with food, clothing, blankets, tools, farm equipment, and building materials. Provincial officers, like their counterparts in the British regiments, received half-pay for life, the payments continuing at a reduced rate if they were survived by widows.

The Survey

To prepare for the arrival of the Loyalists, groups of surveyors and their assistants fanned across the land, subdividing it into small lots for settlement. To provide information for general maps, they were also required to sketch and describe "all ponds, lakes and streams...mountains, hills, and morass" and, at the same time, note the quality of soils and timber. In both provinces the surveyors had to start with clean sheets, working either in unsurveyed country or in country where previous surveys were usually little more than rough outlines of large tracts. As an exercise in surveying and subdivision it would not be matched in nature or scope until the survey and settlement of the American West almost a century later. It was also a pioneer exercise in land allotment and land tenure procedures. To obtain land, a settler, of whatever degree, had to petition the provincial secretary. In turn the secretary would comment on the status of the land (whether vacant or occupied) and on the character of the petitioner (not all petitioners intended to settle) then send the petition to the surveyor-general. From the surveyor-general's office it then went, for approval or rejection, to the Council's committee on land which, in New Brunswick, met almost daily. A petitioner willing to take pot luck had his name registered and either in person, or through an agent or deputy surveyor, drew a lot in newly surveyed territory. Petitioners requesting lots in specific locations were required to advertise in local newspapers for three consecutive weeks and, if there were no rival claimants, the land committee issued a warrant authorizing the surveyor-general to conduct a survey. The warrant and a description of the land surveyed were to be returned to the provincial secretary within six months.

The huge task of providing farm and town lots for the 30,000 Loyalists fell to the surveyor general of lands for each province: Charles Morris for Nova Scotia and George Sproule for New Brunswick. As the son of the first surveyor-general for Nova Scotia and the father and grandfather of his two immediate successors, Charles Morris was part of a century-long surveying dynasty. George Sproule, on the other hand, seems to have been without connections. As a trained army surveyor and engineer who had worked on the first thorough survey of New Hampshire's boundaries, in 1772, his credentials were impeccable. He was appointed surveyor-general for New Hampshire in 1774 but at the outbreak of the Revolutionary War he rejoined the British army. He was appointed surveyor-general for New Brunswick in 1784, a position he held for the next thirty-three years. Edward Winslow, who could be a merciless critic of competence and character, described him as "that correct, faithful & devoted officer."

As managers of the survey, Morris and Sproule delegated the field work to deputy land surveyors. Most of these came from army engineering backgrounds but in an age when land and property were all-important, a knowledge of surveying could be picked up fairly easily. Even so, there were never enough surveyors to satisfy the demand for lots, and in outlying areas the settlers were sometimes authorized to do their own surveying and subdividing. Accompanying each deputy surveyor was an axeman, who cleared lines of sight, and two chain bearers who measured the breadth or width of the lots and ran lines back from the river or shore. In remote or little-known country they were sometimes assigned a Native guide. The surveyor himself worked with a magnetic hand compass and a telescope. Although subject to regional variations in magnetic declination, hand compasses were easy to use and in situations where speed was more important than absolute accuracy they were invaluable.

A deputy-surveyor's chief responsibility was to layout farm lots but the settlement also required town plats, town lots, garden lots, public landings, and government reserves for defence, religion, and education. He also had to survey parish and county lines, check old surveys, vet petitions to the governor, and layout roads. In coastal areas, the roads at first ran along the sandy and sometimes muddy seashores but as the settlement matured they were moved inland to dry banks and ridges. Physically the work of surveying was hard. The ground was often rough and when not thickly wooded it was usually wet or swampy. In warm weather, flies and mosquitoes were constituents of the atmosphere. To add to their trials, surveyors and assistants were required to provide their own food and clothing. For non-surveyors the discomfort was intolerable. Benjamin Marston, a deputy-surveyor, wrote of a customs collector forced (presumably) to share the surveyor's tent: "He won't live long with us, our fare is too hard, our apparatus too indelicate and coarse."

Such was the demand for lots that in the case of group settlements the surveyors were usually reduced to laying out the blocks, leaving the actual subdivision to the groups themselves. The approved method of allocating farm lots that had not been assigned to specific individuals was by a public draw overseen by a deputy surveyor. In theory the method ought to have been fair but in practice some drew blanks when there was supposed to have been enough land for all, while others complained that the tickets drawn did not always correspond with the numbers of the lots in the surveyed district. Through subsequent exchange and sale, both the ownership and the dimensions of lots were frequently changed. Yet however obtained, land grants were subject to improvements that varied according to the nature of the land and which had to be completed within three years. For each fifty acres, the grantee had to clear and cultivate three acres if the land was arable, drain the same amount if it was swampy, sustain three cattle if it was wilderness, or dig a stone quarry if it was rocky. Failure to complete the improvements, as earlier grantees had discovered, exposed the land to recall or escheatment. So great was the crisis posed by the approach of thousands of land-seeking Loyalists that, in an age when property was sacrosanct, government took the bold step of escheating, between 1782 and 1788, two-and-a-half million acres from delinquent grantees.

Landed Estates

In spite of government coolness to the idea of a landed aristocracy in British North America and the spirited resistance of the rank and file to the claims of the Fifty-five, prominent Loyalists still dreamed of a ruling class of landowners. Property and government office, seen then as the only reliable safeguards against age, destitution, and—that worst of all fates—dependence upon relatives, were the twin engines of eighteenth-century society. In an isolated colonial settlement, where government was virtually the only source of a regular income, true reimbursement lay in position and appointments. Land was important as a source of future wealth and as a visible mark of status. Wherever farmable land was available, few men of means could resist the temptation to assemble it and, if they wished to live on it, build country houses. As officers and former landowners, leading Loyalists were entitled to substantial land grants and in most cases these could be augmented by petition and purchase.

The Saint John Valley

Needing farmland, country estates were confined to the major valleys: the Annapolis, the Kennebecasis, and the Saint John. The fertile middle reaches of the Saint John were within easy reach of Fredericton allowing office holders to own a country hut as well as one in town. Even if the country hut was never properly developed it could be given an impressive name. Thus Jacob Ellegood's property at Queensberry above Fredericton became The Manor and Samuel Denny Street's, at Burton, was called Elysian Fields. Ellegood, who had been one of the largest landowners in Virginia, named his townhouse Rose Hall after his Virginia estate. In size and pretension country properties ranged from the modest to the grand. At the modest end of the scale was Dugald Campbell's 580-acre grant on the Nashwaak, a tributary of the Saint John just above Fredericton. On the property Campbell, who was a surveyor and lieutenant in the Royal

Highland Regiment, built a large house from squared timbers, dovetailed at the corners and neatly set in plaster. He named it Taymouth Farm. Campbell had neither the resources nor the time to build a gentleman's estate but his Scottish neighbours, sensing undeclared motives and no doubt piqued at Campbell having taken a disproportionate amount of river frontage, dubbed it Taymouth Castle, the name of the ancient stronghold of the Breadalbane Campbells. Dugald Campbell's branch of the Campbell family were keepers of the forest of Mamlorn, an ancient hereditary office.

At the immodest end of the scale was The Barony, John Saunders' vain attempt to create a fiefdom in the Saint John Valley. Descended from a family of English Cavaliers, Saunders was one of the few Virginia landowners to support the British cause. He responded to the Revolution by raising a troop of horses at his own expense and joining, as a cavalry captain, the Queen's Rangers. After one bloody skirmish in 1781 he is reported to have ordered the execution of a prisoner. His Virginia estate was confiscated and some of his slaves, presumably as punishment for their master's unbending Toryism, are said to have been imprisoned. With no training in law and no reasonable prospect—given the scramble for places—of finding a position within government office in British North America, Saunders left for London and the Inns of Court in 1784. He was called to the bar in 1789 and a year later appointed to a judgeship in the Supreme Court of New Brunswick.

In New Brunswick, Saunders was determined to make amends for the 1,200-acre estate he had forfeited in Norfolk. His commission entitled him to a grant of 1,000 acres and in addition to this he could claim for the property lost in Virginia. But not even doubling his Virginia acreage, as Saunders would argue later, would have made up for differences between the climate and terrain of the two regions. In New Brunswick, where neither land nor climate favoured the farmer, grants of a few hundred or even a thousand acres could do nothing "to excite the ambition or gratify the wishes of men of education, enterprise, or wealth." There were also social implications to the restriction on the size of holdings. Many settled areas of the province were mere congregations of "poor and ignorant men" unable on their own to make improvements. Without well-informed or "respectable" people to advise or control them, it was hardly surprising, Saunders maintained, that "insubordination, immorality, and irreligion prevailed among them, producing effects highly pernicious to society." The remedy, Saunders contended, was to let men of means and ability have as much property as they wanted, provided they could improve it and pay the quitrents.

Making a duty of desire, Saunders began assembling land. Through petition and purchase, and the judicial blocking of rival applications to vacant lots, he ultimately became the greatest landholder in the province. His largest holding was an estate of almost 6,000 acres in Prince William parish about 25 miles above Fredericton. On the Prince William property, Saunders built The Barony, a replica, in wood rather than brick, of his Virginia house. Nearby was The Manor, the property of his brother-in-law and former neighbour in Virginia, Jacob Ellegood. The Barony had a nucleus of island and interval land but most of it was, as one observer remarked, "very bad land." Replenished annually by the silt-laden spring freshets, island and interval soils were not only rich but natural meadowlands which, provided there was enough sun-light between the trees, could be cultivated without clearing. "Upland" soils beyond the reach of the nourishing floodwaters were leached of their nutrients by the heavy rainfall and host to thick growths of conifers. As a rule, uplands were only a fifth to a tenth of the price of island and interval lands.

Captain John Saunders (John Rising, 1789).

New Brunswick Museum

Like every other landowner, Saunders was dogged by a short-age of tenants and labourers. As a result, most of The Barony remained untenanted and unimproved. Saunders had hoped to attract tenants from Europe and his failure to do so, as Colonel Joseph Gubbins noted in 1811, had left the house "in the middle of a wilderness of his own creation, without a neighbour or a practicable road, and his cleared lands...growing again up into forest." In 1819 Saunders was instrumental in the formation of the Fredericton Emigrant Society and six years later he was the founding president of the New Brunswick Agricultural and Emigrant Society. But all to no avail. The province did attract Irish immigrants but most of these, being uneducated and unskilled, were not tenant material. In 1825 the historian Peter Fisher reported that The Barony was still "mostly a wilderness" and that it showed little prospect of improvement. Saunders's English-educated son, John Simcoe Saunders, who considered New Brunswick's "woods and desert air" a poor substitute for life in Oxford and London, was no more optimistic. Indignant at the expectation that he should some day return and manage the estate, he predicted that some future traveller would stumble on it, "like Palmyra in the desert and wonder how the devil it came there." But when he reflected that the house was built of wood, and that the foundation had to be propped up, he thought that even this was "too aspiring an idea." When, on John Simcoe's death in 1878, The Barony was finally put on the market, Moses Perley commented that it was still "a waste howling wilderness" more properly entitled a "barren eh!"

The Barony's elegant, octagonal outhouse. To escape flooding after the building of the Mactaquac dam on the Saint John River in the late 1960s, it was moved to King's Landing Historical Settlement.

Downriver, the largest property was Alwington Manor, a 6,000-acre estate at the mouth of the Nerepis about 12 miles above Saint John. Its owner was the legendary John Coffin who, in an engagement at Eutaw Springs in the Carolinas had led seventy dragoons in a charge against two or three hundred Americans, killing 60 of them, at a cost of only three of his own men, and making prisoners of almost a hundred of the remainder. All the Americans were killed with swords, Coffin disdaining to stop and fire during the execution of the charge. The estate, according to his son Captain Henry Coffin, occupied "a rich and lovely landscape" of hill and dale, magnificent woods, and fine rivers swarming with salmon, bass, and shad that "promised everything to willing hands and stout hearts." The original owner, Colonel Beamsley Glasier, who as the appointed agent for the Saint John River Society had been granted the land in 1769, was just as enthusiastic even though he had done little to improve the grant. He thought the interval lands "wonderful, not a stone and black mold six feet deep, no underwood, large tall trees all hardwood; you may drive a coach through the trees, we can cut what grass we please and may improve the land immediately." In short, continued Glasier, "it looks like a park as far as ever your eye can carry you."

John Coffin bought the land, which was under threat of escheat, for "a trifle," had a house built and in 1784 moved in with his wife, children, and household servants: three black men and one black woman brought from Charleston. Though a sixth generation American, he named the estate Alwington Manor after the Coffin family estate in Devonshire. When Coffin's daughter Caradine built a house on Wolfe's Island near Kingston, Ontario, she also succumbed to ancestor worship, naming her house after the Devonshire estate. Alwington Manor, New Brunswick, could boast no graceful stone mansion, but John Coffin's house was considered grand enough to accommodate the Duke of Kent when he visited the province in 1794.

On Alwington, Coffin had the usual difficulties with labour. The Napoleonic War in Europe had tapped Britain's prospective emigrants and the province, then in an economic slump, could not afford an emigration society of its own. Yet Coffin built saw and grist mills at "enormous outlay," due to the scarcity of labour. By providing stock imported from England and the United States and waiving all returns for the first three years he was, however, able to attract tenants. But the estate still foundered; there are no records chronicling its decline but in 1794 he was fined for selling rum without a licence and when Colonel Gubbins brought news of a promotion in New Brunswick's militia, he found Coffin selling cabbages, delivered by sloop from Alwington, on Saint John's Market slip.

Between Alwington and The Barony there were a number of estates, all within easy reach of Fredericton. Closest to town was the Governor's "Farm," a 1,000-acre property on which Governor Carleton built, with his own funds, a large house and garden. On his visit to New Brunswick in 1794 a magnanimous Duke of Kent declared that the view from the terrace "exceeded that of Windsor Castle." A description of the house by its subsequent occupant, Lady Sir Martin Hunter, suggests that the Duke was not exaggerating. She found the house "large and commodious, with one most magnificent room." With a terrace and a charming garden maintained in "the highest imaginable order" overlooking the river, its situation, too, was "the finest in the world...as to the picturesque and romantic."

The governor's property, however, was more than a picturesque showpiece. Below the garden fine pastures sloped down to the river while behind the house, on 400 acres rented from the College of New Brunswick, he conducted

Colonel John Coffin's house at Westfield on the Saint John River (George Neilson Smith, 1839).

New Brunswick Museum

what amounted to an experimental farm. There, he raised what is said to have been central New Brunswick's first herd of cattle, and grew crops, trees, and shrubs with seeds and cuttings brought from England and the United States. Like most well-born eighteenth-century Englishmen he considered agriculture to be more important than commerce and he was determined that Fredericton should be an agricultural centre as well as an administrative and military one. Because seeds and cuttings were valued gifts in a pioneer society, the governor's successful transplants spread quickly through the province.

Governor Thomas Carleton's residence, Fredericton, destroyed by fire in 1825.

About thirty miles upriver from Fredericton, at the mouth of the swift-flowing Pokiok, was Kingswood, Edward Winslow's country property from which he hoped to make money from milling lumber as well as farming. Winslow, however, had chosen some of the least farmable land in the area. He made little money from the property and little, too, from public service despite a life that balanced solicitude with relentless office-seeking. A Supreme Court judgeship, awarded in his last years despite his lack of any formal training in law, brought some financial relief but as the father of fourteen children he was never able to clear old debts accumulated by the free-spending Winslow family before the Revolutionary War. He died heavily in debt and lies in an unmarked grave in Fredericton's Loyalist cemetery.

About ten miles downstream from Kingsclear and five above Fredericton was Springhill, the "valuable and elegant" seat of Chief Justice George Duncan Ludlow. Ludlow's holdings, of which Springhill was the largest, amounted to just over 3,000 acres, making him one of the largest landowners in the area. On islands in the river below the house Patrick Campbell saw the "rankest" (finest) crops of any country he was ever in: gardens bursting with onions, beets, and squash, and chest-high crops of wheat and rye in fields that had never seen a single shovelful of manure. Bishop Charles Inglis, who dined at Springhill in 1788, found the house "very neat [and] convenient," sheltered by fine large forest trees, and offering pleasing prospects of the river. As a former forester who deplored the Loyalist preference for imported mahogany furniture, Patrick Campbell congratulated Ludlow on his use of "the beautiful native woods." Ludlow's son, however, for whom life in London and Paris precluded appreciation of anything local, advertised the property in 1811 after his father, through sales to neighbours, had reduced it to about half of its original size. In addition to a fine and commodious house he offered "fifteen hundred acres of excellent land, part of it in orchard, mowing ground and arable land, the remainder in fine timber of maple, birch, elm, butter-nut." The property was rented by Lieutenant-Colonel Gubbins, an English career officer who, between his tours of inspection of the New Brunswick militia, is said to have lived the life of a country gentleman.

For Southern Loyalists, in particular, the life of a country gentleman would have seemed incomplete without Black or slave labour. Jacob Ellegood, at Queensbury, and Stair Agnew, on a property at the mouth of the Nashwaak, both Virginians, persisted in adhering, as one observer put it euphemistically, "to the rights of property exercised in the Southern States." After a court case in 1790 initiated by two high-minded lawyers (Ward Chipman and Samuel Denny) to test the legality of slavery, the panel of four judges was divided. Two found for the slaveholder and two for the slave. Infuriated by the trial, Agnew

Overleaf: Springhill. This nineteenth-century George Heriot painting is a Georgian idyl: a classically-proportioned mansion house, expansive fields and meadows shaded by leafy deciduous trees, grazing or slumbering animals, and a haycart followed by the mounted stewards of the property.

Royal Ontario Museum

challenged Judge Isaac Allen—one of the two judges who sided with slave Nancy Morton—to a duel. Allen declined the challenge but, sticking to his precepts, freed his own slaves. Agnew kept his; however, like other slaveholders he would have learned that Black slaves—who were regularly sold at public auction in Saint John—could be used only as domestic servants. There were few field hands or common labourers among them and, like the freed Blacks who greatly outnumbered them, they had no liking for the cold Maritime climate. Some of the freed Blacks did work on farms, and a few even farmed for themselves, but most of the farmers and labourers were lost when a scheme to create a self-governing colony of free Blacks in Sierra Leone went into effect in 1791.

By 1795, the shortage of tenants and labour was so pressing a problem for estate owners that Stair Agnew, at a public meeting in Van Horne's Tavern in Fredericton, could declare a heresy: that landowners would be better off if the province were annexed to the United States. Lands, he asserted, would become more valuable and labour cheaper. In an effort to raise money from the sale of crown lands in 1790, the British government, declared a ban on the granting of free land in New Brunswick, inadvertently creating an image of a province that was unfriendly to immigrants. Defeated by the shortage of labour and tenants, Agnew began to sell parts of his property, Monkton, in 1813 and after his death in 1821 his family sold or lost the remainder.

The Kennebecasis Valley

At the time of Patrick Campbell's visit in 1793, the Kennebecasis Valley, although slower to attract settlers than the Saint John Valley, was regarded as one of the most favoured parts of the province: "the fittest for new settlers, the easiest land to clear, and for raising stock with least trouble." Loyalists moved into the valley from Saint John, slowly at first because the lower Kennebecasis is too rough for farming, but above Hampton the valley softens into a smiling vale that the French had earlier earmarked as a location for seigneurial estates. Today it is one of the few truly pastoral regions of New Brunswick. In the section known as Pleasant Valley, a broad flat or interval between Salmon and Trout Creeks—the two headwater streams of the Kennebecasis—Colonel George Leonard, the provincial Superintendent of Trade and Fisheries, acquired a 2,000-acre property. On it he built Rosemount, a "genteel house," which he set in grounds planted with roses and other flowering shrubs. Furniture, paintings, silver plate, books, and ornaments were all brought from New England. Bishop Charles Inglis, who stayed at Rosemount on one of his tours of the diocese, said that the house reminded him of a European villa.

As well as embellishing the property, Leonard also improved it. Some of the land he rented to "the peasantry", as he described them. He provided tenants with tools, seed, and animals on the understanding that at the end of a three-year lease, profits would be divided equally. Patrick Campbell thought the arrangement an ideal stepping stone for penniless immigrants who one day hoped to own their own farms. Attracted to the methods of English high farming, Leonard worked at improving breeds of cattle and methods of cultivation. English methods were not always applicable to New Brunswick yet there is some evidence that

A sketch of Rosemount, George Leonard's country house near Sussex, New Brunswick.

New Brunswick Museum

English agricultural texts were preferred to American. Charles Turner, an American surveyor and outspoken commentator, chided Major Benjamin Griffiths, a landowner near Woodstock, for surrounding himself with English books on agriculture and gardening and ignoring "that good old pedagogue: Experience." The major's practices, wrote a nonplussed Turner, were at war with every principle of reason and common sense. Ignoring such "trifling circumstances" as differences in climate and soil "he nobly soars above the whole, and places his labor and seed where, when, and as his books direct." Had Turner visited Prince Edward Island he might also have rebuked the farmers there for growing wheat instead of the more suitable oats and potatoes. In Sussex, George Leonard also adopted English equipment, but not always successfully. He employed an itinerant millwright to make a threshing machine from a description he had obtained from England but when completed, as Lieutenant-Colonel Gubbins remarked, "the flails struck in all directions."

In spite of his efforts, Leonard, like most other estate owners, lost heavily. Gubbins reported that Rosemount cost Leonard £8,000 to clear and get in order, but in 1811, following a collapse of land values in New Brunswick, it would have sold for only £3,000. A few miles downstream, near what is now the village of Apohaqui, Gilfred Studholme, the retired commander of the Saint John garrison and former Deputy Surveyor-General of Nova Scotia, was no more successful. His estate, Studville, was a "very valuable" 2,000-acre grant that, by paralleling the river and running "very little distance back," took up an inordinate amount of river frontage. By contravening a central principle of colonial land allotment, the arrangement was "not agreeable to his majesty's orders" but this did not prevent Studholme from occupying and developing the land. He built a house overlooking the river, operated a sawmill, and attempted to grow hemp, then in great demand by the Maritime ship-rope trade. But by 1790 both his milling and hemp-growing schemes were in trouble and he declared himself "very hard drove for money." Dogged by ill-health, he died prematurely in 1792, and following his death, the estate reverted to the crown. In 1798 it was gifted to Colonel James Chalmers, the father-in-law of John Saunders, and when Colonel Chalmers died in 1806 part of it fell to the Saunders estate.

Although he had little money—at the time of probate the estate was valued at only £350 pounds—Gilfred Studholme lived the life of an English country gentleman. He owned fine pieces of furniture, elegant table silver, various decanters and glasses, an extensive library that included works by Virgil, Montaigne, Rousseau, and Milton and a wardrobe described as large, stylish, and commodious. His stock of clothes consisted of eighteen silk or velvet waistcoats, some of them embroidered, several pairs of silk breeches and stockings, various overcoats and jackets, and jewellry that included a tortoise shell snuffbox, paste shoe buckles set in silver, a gold brooch, and a set of gold enamelled sleeve buttons.

In spite of Studholme's experiments with hemp and his obvious lack of wealth, estates in the Saint John and Kennebecasis Valleys were developed not for promoting the interest of the province in matters such as land policy and economic development. They were a way of leading a coveted way of life but to maintain them their owners had to rely on income from a government office or a pension. A notable exception was Wills Knox, son of Under-Secretary William Knox. Until his retirement in 1808, William Knox was also the provincial agent for New Brunswick in London and as a reward a grateful Assembly voted him a sum of money. To keep the money in the province he bought 5,000 acres in the Kennebecasis Valley. When he died in 1809 the property, in the parish of Norton, passed to his son Wills. The younger Knox, applying English standards of land assessment, imagined himself so well-provided for that he left the British East India Company and came to New Brunswick with his furniture and his servants. However, his illusions were shattered quickly and he was reduced to selling off his belongings. At the time of Colonel Gubbins' visit, in July 1811, Knox was trying to give some of his worthless land to his servants in the hope that they might improve it enough to make the remainder saleable.

The Head of the Bay

Outside the Saint John and Kennebecasis Valleys, New Brunswick's only size-able area of flat, cultivable land was the marshland, formerly occupied by Acadians, at the head of the Bay of Fundy. Though rich and easily cultivated, distance from the Loyalist heartland and uncertainties over land tenure in the marshlands and surrounding uplands deterred settlement. Among the roughly 200 Loyalists attracted to the area was Amos Botsford, one of seven agents appointed to arrange for the settlement of Loyalists in the old province of Nova Scotia. Until the Revolution, Botsford, a graduate of Yale, had been a prominent lawyer in New Haven. After the division of the province and a falling out with Charles Morris and Governor Parr, he moved across the bay from Digby to the mouth of the Memramcook River. But his property there proved difficult to farm and in 1790, he acquired 800 acres of the underused Westcock Marsh near Sackville. On the upland overlooking his dyked fields and the Nova Scotian shore he built, from brick, a Georgian mansion house. With a pediment-like gable over the entrance, a "pretty" dining room, a large drawing room, a book-lined library, wide halls, and sunny bedrooms—all furnished with imported pieces from England and New England—it was said to have been as fine a house as any in New Brunswick.

The grounds were also enchanting. In a letter to his son, Botsford wrote proudly of a "remarkably beautiful" flower garden with an array of *fleurs-de-lis*, peonies in full bloom, and a profusion of honeysuckle and white lupin, all protected by a quickset hedge. Many years later, in a novel set in Westcock, Charles G.D. Roberts referred to the "horse chestnuts and Lombardy poplars that ranged magnificently before the old home, and the sudden waft of perfume from a deep thicket of blossoming lilacs in the back field of Westcock House."

Botsford's marshland estate was more durable than most. The tent and cabin city of Saint John required large quantities of grain, meat, and vegetables and Botsford was well-placed to take advantage of the demand. The marsh yielded rich crops of wheat, oats, and potatoes as well as hay and grazing for cattle and sheep. And being on the edge of the bay, its produce could be shipped directly and cheaply to Saint John. Cattle were also marketed on the hoof. To speed delivery of the large numbers of cattle and sheep needed by the new settlements, Thomas Carleton pressed for the construction of a highway. Work began in 1786 and before the end of the decade, cattle were being driven over the Westmoreland Road linking Sackville and Saint John. Although the Botsford estate was eventually divided and sold, the excellent land, the accessibility of the Saint John market, and the availability of casual Acadian and immigrant Yorkshire labour gave it staying power. "Law and farming," Botsford advised his son William, who inherited the estate, "will answer here."

The Annapolis Valley

Loyalist estates in Nova Scotia were confined to one of the few areas of fertile land not previously claimed by the New England Planters. More interested in the rich coastlands of the Minas Basin than in inland place, the Planters had overlooked the the upper reaches of the Annapolis River. With no roads to the interior, valley lands above Annapolis were comparatively remote, and few settlers were willing to give up the safety and comfort of older townships. There was some movement into the interior, but no real influx until after the Revolution. Among those Loyalists hoping to settle in the valley was 74-year-old Timothy Dwight Ruggles, a graduate of Harvard, a lawyer, a member and Speaker of the Massachusetts Assembly, and a Brigadier-General in command of a Loyalist regiment. On his estate at Hardwick, Massachusetts, where he kept a deer park and raised hunters and hounds, Ruggles lived the life of a country squire.

In Nova Scotia, Ruggles applied for a grant that reflected his station: 10,000 acres in the Annapolis Basin near Granville. Much of the land in the Granville area had already been taken up and the rest was to be divided into small farm lots that would give each settler a section of coveted river land as well as upland. Charles Morris, the surveyor-general, objected vehemently to the application, which he thought would both "disgust the people" and prove "very injurious to the settlement in general," and he refused to recommend it. Ruggles, very much affronted, appealed directly to Governor Parr who, backing Morris, offered Ruggles 10,000 acres in the less-settled township of Wilmot. Though still indignant, Ruggles accepted the offer and moved to Wilmot with his slaves and two of his sons. The latter were awarded contiguous 800-acre grants at the back of their father's estate. Ruggles's own grant extended from the Annapolis River to the Fundy shore. On it, he began building a house, a "roomy affair" on a foundation of dressed Quincy granite brought from Massachusetts. The house was never finished but the estate is said to have featured the district's model farm.

A passionate horticulturist, Ruggles planted the township's first apple orchard with young trees brought from Massachusetts. In a warm, deep cleft on the south-facing hillside he also grew peaches, grapes, quinces, and a black walnut tree. From the first he recognized the Valley's affinity for fruits and vegetables. In a letter to Edward Winslow, he spoke of apples (from trees planted by Acadians or Planters) as fine and fair as any seen in New York, of vegetables of the very best quality and, quoting Colonel Allen of Jersey, of cider the like of which had never before been pressed. The problems of developing and managing a 10,000-acre estate were, of course, never properly addressed by the ageing general. In exchange for grants of 500 acres each he acquired for three years the services of two young men who, with the help of Colonel Ruggles's slaves, planted his orchards and gardens and cleared space for the never finished mansion house. Ruggles also hired soldiers to do some of the heavy work but the problem of labour was never resolved. After his death in 1795, his son John sold much of the estate, including the part with the house. His other son Richard sold his grant and moved to the village of Clements.

Ruggles's neighbour in the Valley was Charles Inglis, the first colonial bishop and a prominent member of the Committee of Fifty-five. Through marriage, Inglis had acquired land in the Hudson Valley in New York and, by having to manage it, the skills of estate mangement. On coming to Nova Scotia, he bought the 5,000-acre property of Captain David Phipps—who had returned to England—and through purchase and land grants between 1787 and 1791 he doubled the original acreage. On a small sheltered rise he built a one-and-a-half- storey farmhouse, laid out an extensive garden; and planted an orchard with trees imported from New York.

Named "Clermont" after a well-known manor in the Hudson Valley, the Inglis estate was by far the most successful in Nova Scotia. A serious farmer and horticulturist, Inglis deplored the farming methods of the New England settlers, which he considered slipshod and unscientific. Like George Leonard on the Kennebecasis, he encouraged crop rotation and the proper breeding and feeding of cattle. In 1789 he was also instrumental in founding a society for promoting agriculture in Nova Scotia, which, despite its small population, was forced to import food from the United States. At Clermon, Inglis practiced what he preached, continually experimenting with new agricultural methods and, as a skilled horticulturist, with new hybrids. Using shoots and cuttings from Massachusetts and New York, he and General Ruggles developed strains of apple adapted to the Nova Scotia climate. Inglis is associated with a number of hybrid Nova Scotian varieties but he is best known for his "Bellefleur" or "Bishop Pippin."

Inglis had the usual difficulties with labour. He complained of the "unparalleled indolence" and "knavish disposition" of the local people but by 1791 he had serviced the estate with roads and bridges, on one occasion paying in rum just to get the work done. Through what observers described as a "progressive tenantry," he also managed to attract tenants—in return for the loan of two yoke of oxen, a milk cow, a calf, and a horse, his tenants gave up a percentage of their crops and after an agreed number of years had to return stock of the same age and value. Tenants, too, had to clear an agreed number of acres and work on the roads running through their lots. For settlers without cash, a lease with an ample supply of stock could be more attractive than free land without it. By 1791 Inglis had managed to attract eight tenants, but the Napoleonic War brought immigration to a halt and with it any hope of attracting new settlers. Inglis died before the end of the war but his son, John, who took over management of the estate, was able to benefit from the revival of immigration that followed the peace. At John Inglis's death, in 1850, the estate had 53 tenants.

Just beyond the Annapolis Valley, about midway between Windsor and Halifax, is the remnant of one of Nova Scotia's largest country estates. Legend has it that, while being escorted to Halifax to face trial for joining a 1776 Patriot attack on Fort Cumberland, Richard John Uniacke begged the escorting sergeant to remove his shackles so that he might savour a stretch of country that reminded him of his family's estate in Ireland. The resemblance between Nova Scotia and County Cork could only have been fancied, but the Irish sergeant obliged, and after a turn through the woods, Uniacke vowed to return and build a house. Through the intervention of powerful family friends and an agreement to take the oath of allegiance, the "great lubbery insolent Irish rebel," as Winslow characterized him, escaped the charges of treason. He became a successful lawyer and, through the genius of Nova Scotia politics, advocate general of the vice admiralty court and attorney general for the province.

In 1813, rich and full of honours, Uniacke returned to the Windsor road. Through grants and purchase, he assembled an estate of 11,000 acres only 500 acres of which, by his own admission, could be cultivated. Even this, according to his biographer Brian Cuthbertson, was an exaggeration. He spent freely on clearing and farming and bought books on agriculture and applied science, but unlike Bishop Inglis and General Ruggles, Uniacke seems to have been more interested in a fine house, landscaped grounds, and a prospect than in farming or horticulture. He cultivated some property and imported cattle to graze on

Uniacke House, 1956. The house was bought by the Government of Nova Scotia in 1949 and opened as a museum in 1952.

Public Archives of Nova Scotia

the rest. The view from the house is toward a lake, and the view from the post road from Windsor to Halifax (which ran close to the property) is of the house's majestic portico. Behind the portico lie other classic Georgian features: a wide central hallway that bisects the house and separates dining room and library from drawing room and a bedroom. The furniture for these and the seven bedrooms on the second floor was made to order, in solid mahogany, by the English furniture maker George Adams.

The Landscape of Fact

With the exception of the Inglises at Clermont and the Botsfords at Westcock, the reign of the estate and the gentleman farmer was quickly over. Land had little intrinsic value and without labourers or tenants to work it, the estates were an embarrassment to be broken up quickly by the children or grandchildren into farms of sizes that could be handled by a single family. John Saunders complained of the "very great scarcity of labourers" that limited the improvements he could make to The Barony. But not only had he miscalculated the liberating effect of the frontier he had also, like several of his fellow estate owners, made the mistake of preferring quantity to quality in his parcels of land. In an "elegant cottage," but six miles from The Barony, noted the merciless Lady Sir Martin Hunter, lived a Mr Aligood. With fewer than 100 acres in tillage and pasture "he raises more cattle and grows more grain than the Judge in all his immense estate." When twelve to fifteen acres was as much as the average family could plant and harvest in a year, and with 100- or 200-acre grants available for the asking, who would be a labourer or even a tenant?

Even when labour and tenants were available they were a mixed blessing. Colonel Stephen Kemble, the proprietor of one of the few Saint John River Society grants to survive the Loyalist settlement, told his attorney that it was more important to keep tenants in good humour than to force them to the terms of their contracts. During 1788, Colonel Kemble, a career soldier, had charge of Kemble Manor, the family estate near Hampstead. So great was the need for Blacks who had neither land of their own nor access to government provisions. Some became labourers and some became share croppers or tenant farmers who gave up half of their produce. It was a system akin, as the visiting English abolitionist John Clarkson remarked, to "a state of slavery." One of the landowners was Bishop Inglis who had one Black tenant, John Brown. Brown's eight-acre plot was "in better order, neater, and more flourishing than any of the others," but this, Clarkson noted, did not deter the bishop from moving him to another part of the estate, there to begin all over again. Other landowners employed common soldiers hired out by officers who then collected their wages. Cobbett took a dim view of the practice and attempted to lay charges against the offending officers after his discharge in England in 1791.

With all classes having to work, social barriers came down but not, as it sometimes appeared to English observers, to the ground. Lord Edward Fitzgerald, a major in the 54th Regiment who arrived in Halifax in 1788 and made his way around the head of the Bay of Fundy to Saint John, found that he liked "the equality of everybody and...their manner of life. There are no gentlemen; everybody is on a footing (provided he works) and wants nothing; every man is exactly what he can make himself, or is made by industry." The levelling effect of the frontier, that the American historian Frederick Jackson Turner would fashion into a celebrated thesis, had also been noted by Colonel Gubbins on his tours of inspection of the New Brunswick militia. But whereas Turner, an American democrat, applauded the change, Gubbins, an English Tory, deplored it. With labour everywhere in short supply, virtually everyone, Gubbins noted regretfully, had to work. "The sons of the officers of rank and of other gentlemen who took refuge here after the American war, though many of them have received tolerable education and are gentlemanlike in their manners... are obliged to undergo the drudgery of farming." Hard and relentless physical labour worked inexorably against education and manners; daughters and sons being neither as refined nor as well-read as their parents. Not even settlers raised in England were immune to the coarsening effects of the frontier. Compelled to make a living with their axes, as Gubbins put it, they soon lost their English manners and, in remote places, "degenerated very rapidly into a state of barbarism."

But not all British observers were disturbed by the change. Patrick Campbell referred matter-of-factly to captains as black as colliers and to British half-pay officers with a few cows having to milk them with their own hands, lay by the milk, make the churn, muck the byre, and sweep the kitchen. Unable to afford a single servant, they did all the drudgery themselves or let it go untended. Though an outspoken critic of republicanism, Cobbett, as a lowly NCO, clearly exulted in the reversal of roles: "Thousands of Captains and Colonels without soldiers" and "squires without stockings or shoes" from whom, moreover, he could demand service. In England he would never have approached a squire without a respectful bow, but in the new world, he wrote, "I often ordered a squire to bring me a glass of grog, and even to take care of my knapsack."

Although a few of the estates survived well into the nineteenth century, it was the small, independent farm that dominated areas of Loyalist settlement in New Brunswick and Nova Scotia. Except for the block settlements for the disbanded regiments, none of which succeeded, there were no plans to build communities as there had been in New England and in the Planter settlements of Nova Scotia. Even in the case of small, closely-knit groups, settlement was dispersed from the outset. The Bellisle Creek of the Saint John River at Kingston was settled by a group of Anglicans from neighbouring communities in southwest Connecticut. For several years they had lived together as refugees on Long Island, but on the Bellisle each family lived on its long and narrow river lot, rather than more compactly in a village. The families shared a church and a school, but neither Kingston nor any of the other Loyalist settlements were villages in the Old World or seventeenth-century New England sense.

In the country, as in the towns, strict order prevailed. The smaller lots ran in narrow sections back from the rivers or the coast, the rear or base line of the lots paralleling the course of the river or the shore. In the absence of roads all lots had to be near water. In a 1785 warrant for a survey on the Bellisle Creek, George Sproule instructed the deputy surveyor that he was not to lay out lots "higher than a boat can go at this season." If extra lots were needed they were laid out behind the first concession of lots and to give their occupants access to the water road allowances were left at convenient intervals between the lots in the front tier. Throughout the colonies a leading principle of land allocation was that lands did not extend in length along navigable waterways. In his 1839 instructions to his deputy surveyors, which must

Farm lots outside Kingston, New Brunswick, c. 1906. In the distance is the village and the spire of Trinity Church.

Public Archives of New Brunswick

Kingston village, c. 1906. In the background is the Belleisle Creek.

Public Archives of New Brunswick

have followed established precedent, John Spry Morris advised that when, "laying out allotments bounded by harbours, navigable waters, rivers with intervale lands, ensure that allotments are five times as deep as they are wide."

The dimensions of the tracts depended on the topography and on the number of settlers to be accommodated in a given area. In extreme cases lots could be as narrow as 88 yards (16 rods) and as long as seven miles but a typical 200-acre farm might have 440 yards of frontage with the concession stretching back 2,200 yards. Where the ground was underwater or badly drained surveyors compensated by increasing the size of the holding and, as a general rule, added 10 percent to the prescribed acreages to compensate for road allowances and waste lands. In theory, a farmer could live any-where on his holding but most built their houses near the river or the shore or, if on the second tier of lands back from the river, near the road. The sys-tem clearly discouraged the growth of compact villages. A typical farming set-tlement consisted of a string of houses and barns, along a winding road or river, interrupted occasionally by a church, a school, or a store.

The chance nature of the pattern ran counter to the eighteenth-century sense of order, and the long narrow lots—whose back sections were so far from river or road as to be unuseable—the sense of efficiency. In many cases, settlers sold off the back portions of their lots and, to increase their river or lake frontage, bought their neighbours' lots. But even if soils had been cultivable throughout the lot, the tendency would have been to cultivate only the land within easy reach of the road or river. Back from the rivers, soils tended to be sandy or stony, acid or sour, and covered with conifers.

Dwellings and Living Standards

The first farm houses were simple structures. Only the rich could build solidly and comfortably from the start, and hire carpenters and labourers if any were available. Far from the ports and British supplies, settlers were forced to build from the materials at hand: logs at first, then hand-hewn timber and boards. Log houses were sometimes clapboarded or shingled and the interiors panelled with planed boards. When sawn lumber and stone became available, or could be

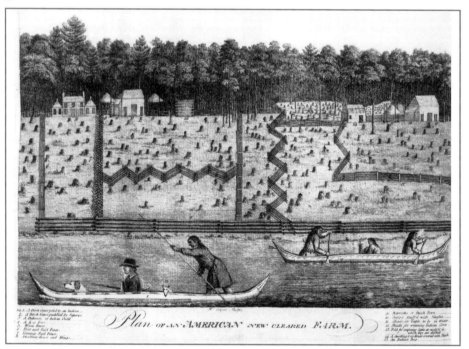

A sketch of newly cleared river lots from Patrick Campbell's Travels in the Interior Inhabited Parts of North America, *1793.*

afforded, log and hand-hewn timber cabins were replaced by permanent houses, usually frame but occasionally of brick or stone. What is now popularly regarded as the characteristic Loyalist farmhouse was a two-storeyed gable house with a central door and hallway, and windows in the upper level set directly above those below. Whether in the country or the town, Loyalist houses tended to be models of symmetry and proportion.

Most farm families lived modestly—even meagrely. The number of acres cleared varied considerably, ranging from fewer than 10 up to (in exceptional cases) more than 50. In an 1827 report on emigration, Alexander Wedderburn

A plain folk or vernacular house, built c.1820, in the Saint John Valley below Fredericton. The kitchen/storehouse extension appears to have been an afterthought.

Public Archives of New Brunswick

noted that the amount of clearing depended on the "internal force" of a family. A moderately determined and energetic family might have had 12 to 15 acres cleared and perhaps a half dozen cattle, a horse, and a few sheep. Only farms on the intervals required little if any clearing. Henry Nase, an ex-ensign and diarist who settled near the confluence of the Nerepis and the Saint John in 1783 and was lucky enough to get interval land, makes no reference to burning off the bush until 1794. Nase may have been lucky in his allotment but, as the historian Esther Clark Wright pointed out, he quickly learned the lesson of the country. "I have four fine boys," he wrote in a letter to Edward Winslow, "and have no other means of providing for them but learn them to work and make them farmers." As in all pioneer settlements, the keys to success were drive and self-sufficiency. "A division of labour does not answer well in a new country," noted a visitor to the Loyalist settlements of Prince Edward Island in 1825. On the Island, as elsewhere, the Loyalists built their own houses, did their own

A two-storey farmhouse, now regarded as the characteristic Loyalist type. Standard features were five windows across the front, a medium pitched roof with no eaves, and a central door and hallway. Built in 1812 for Daniel Moorhouse from Connecticut, the house is now at King's Landing Historical Settlement.

Private collection

joiner work, mason work, glazing, and painting while the women spun, knit, and wove linens and woolen cloth.

Only where soils were rich and markets available did farmers live well, supplementing fare from the kitchen garden and the fields with game from the woods and fish from the rivers. Cobbett's representative Loyalist farmer, probably from the Nashwaak, could have been found in any of the major valleys: "an easy and happy farmer," and "one of those Yankee Loyalists who invariably provided a table loaded with good things." Cobbett's assessment was confirmed by Lady Sir Martin Hunter on her journey up the Saint John River to Fredericton. She noted that the farms had a good many cattle, sheep, and horses and that the people were "well fed, well clothed, comfortably lodged, and contented." A few farmers, too, managed to live with some elegance. When staying in the country near Woodstock, Charles Turner, the American surveyor, was astonished to see—in a place settled so recently—a group of finely dressed young men and women prepared, after a quilting session, to spend the evening dancing. The women, all dressed in white, "performed their parts in the style and taste of Boston."

Soldier Settlements

One of the most pressing problems for governments in the aftermath of war is how to employ disbanded soldiers. At the end of the Revolutionary War, officers and men from what remained of the Loyalist regiments were free to do as they pleased. Some took "French leave" and went their own way without bothering to go through the formality of a discharge. Others gathered at the embarkation

Rusagonis, a Loyalist farmhouse.

ports to await formal discharge either in the port or, more commonly, on their arrival at one of the Loyalist settlements. For different reasons, both Sir Guy Carleton and Edward Winslow, Sir Guy's appointee as land agent for the Loyalist regiments, were intent on keeping the remnants of the regiments— perhaps one quarter or less of their original strength—intact. Sir Guy's motives were military, whereas Winslow's were chiefly societal.

By settling each regiment on a single block of land, and employing a gradu- ated system of land grants based on rank, Winslow hoped to keep alive the dream of a land-based civil hierarchy and, at the same time, preserve good order. Large bodies of men more familiar with weapons than tools, and unused to the routines of work, are a threat to any society and to a frontier one in particular. In Nova Scotia and New Brunswick there was an additional haz- ard: the disbanded soldiers had access to a virtual pipeline of cheap West Indian rum. Jealous of their control over land grants and determined not to be confronted with a large group of even sober Loyalist soldiers, officials in Halifax had no intention of accommodating Winslow's design. Apart from the social and political threat posed by large blocks of disbanded soldiers, it was common knowledge among colonial officials that soldiers make the worst pos- sible pioneers. "Of all men," Governor Lawrence concluded after his experi- ence with "King's Bad Bargains" at Halifax, "soldiers were the least qualified to establish new countries." Every soldier who had come to this province, he reported to the Lords of Trade and Plantations, had either quit "or become a Dram Seller." Yet grants of land remained a standard method of rewarding military service. A recruiting bill for a Loyalist regiment in 1777 read: "such spirited fellows who are willing to engage will be rewarded at the End of the war...with 50 Acres of Land, where every gallant Hero may retire and enjoy his Bottle and his Lass."

In peninsular Nova Scotia, scattered blocks of land were granted to about 3,000 disbanded Loyalist and British soldiers. Most of the blocks, however, which had never been inspected and surveyed, were seldom attractive enough to induce the soldiers to stay. In some cases, the farm lots were so far from the townsites that soldiers who, after the New England fashion, were awarded both a town lot and a farm lot were forced to give up one or the other. At Chedabucto the lots of the 60th regiment and the Duke of Cumberland's South Carolina regiment were between five and twenty-five miles from New Manchester (later renamed Guysborough), and at Town Point (later renamed Dorchester) on the North Shore the town and farm lots of the Nova Scotia Volunteers were six miles apart.

More often than not, the farm lots were unfarmable. After spending the winter of 1783-4 hutted in the woods, the men of the 38th and 40th regiments were offered "rock gardens" at Clements. Often the site designated for settlement had nothing to recommend it but a bay or a harbour. At Port Mouton, settled initially by 125 members of Banastre Tarleton's British legion, even this was shallow, sandy, and stormy. For at least half a mile behind the shore the land is—as it must also have been in 1784—littered with granite and whinstone rocks and covered with scrub spruce, poplar, and wire birch. Port Mouton would have been a cruel fate for any refugees, but for a group accustomed to the rich soils and warm climate of the Carolinas it was purgatory. When the Legion arrived in the cold, wet October of 1783, Lieutenant Thomas Scott and Surgeon Edward Smith took one look at the landscape, hired a shallop, and headed for Liverpool. But the rest, who were joined during the remainder of a particularly cold October and November by 2,000 New York-based personnel of the British Army and Navy, hung on only to have their primitive settlement destroyed by fire the following spring.

Unable or unwilling to farm rock gardens or barren shores, many of the soldier grantees moved quickly into the towns and, in the case of the disbanded British soldiers, out of the country altogether. Particularly footloose were the single, unattached men. When Governor Parr visited Guysborough County in March 1788 he found that "many of the privates [had] sold their Lotts foe a dollar or a pair of Shoes—or a few pounds of Tobacco—but most for a gallon of New England Rum and quit the Country without taking any residence." Others took to lumbering, fishing, and trading, sometimes combining these with farming, and in some cases losing their entitlement to rations because they were not clearing their farms. In June 1784 when William Shaw arrived for the muster at Country Harbour, he found the soldiers building boats for the fisheries, not clearing and settling their grants. Few of the soldiers would have had any experience of fishing but the fish were so plentiful that even novices could catch enough for their own needs.

Returns from farming were much slower. Only where the soils were rich and the soldiers resolute did the military settlements resemble anything approaching stability. One of Nova Scotia's few successes was the "soldiers' grant" on Hants County's East River where the rich bottomland or interval soils were alluring enough to entice settlers inland, and productive enough to enable them to stay. Until they blazed a trail, there were no paths to neighbouring settlements and seeds and supplies had to be hauled in on their backs or, in winter, on sleds. Sober, industrious, and even serious, they are said to have been very different from disbanded soldiers in general.

North of the Bay of Fundy, to which Winslow turned when the Halifax government rejected his plans for peninsular Nova Scotia, most of the disbanded or disbanding soldiers were assigned to the Saint John Valley. For Winslow, a rich valley distant from Halifax had immediate appeal and it was there in July 1783 that he suggested that Nova Scotia be divided. With no government officials to restrain him, he resolved to place the regiments on adjoining blocks in the upper reaches of the valley above Fredericton. Winslow's objective was to convert the blocks into a county and by appointing county magistrates from among the officers reduce the possibility of civil disorder. He was anxious that the men, as he put it, "should feel the more delicate restraint of civil authority" before losing "their ideas of military subordination." The most gentlemanly province on earth could not be defiled by drunken and licentious soldiery.

But in New Brunswick, as in ancient Rome, there were military as well as social and administrative reasons for keeping the command structures intact. Colonial experience to the contrary, both Sir Guy Carleton and officials in London subscribed to the belief that ex-soldiers make desirable colonists, capable of developing a country in peace and defending it in time of war. In case of attack, groups of veteran soldiers assigned to farmlands along vulnerable frontiers should, in theory, provide a valuable first line of defence. Sir Guy hoped that land could be allocated in such a way as to resemble "the cantonments of an army, with such distinction of favour to the officers as will enable them to preserve their authority and collect the whole if need should require." Americans were not rattling their sabres in 1784 but soldier settlements on or near the American border would be bound to discourage expansionist sentiments. Sir Guy Carleton indicated a preference for settlements along the St. Croix, which in southern New Brunswick formed the international boundary, but left the final decision to Loyalist agents in the field. Under instructions "to take up a tract of land sufficient to accommodate all the Officers and Men of the Provincial Regiments," these had no hesitation in choosing the Saint John.

The plans for New Brunswick's soldier settlements called for a block 12 miles square—a township—to be assigned to each regiment. The terminology suggests that there might have been expectations of a town or village developing in the centre of each of the "12-mile tracts," as the blocks were afterwards known, but whatever the expectations the plans were never realized. The regimental groups varied too much in size for settlement by regular blocks to be practical, and in a land without roads the general desire for river frontage meant the tracts were divided, as in the civilian settlements, into narrow lots at right angles to the rivers.

There is some evidence that officers got the best land and the best-shaped lots. On his visit to the Nashwaak in 1805 the Reverend James McGregor noted that the men, assigned to lots that were "all length and no breadth" in the narrowest parts of the valley, "had been miserably abused in their settlement." The officers' lots, on the other hand, were in the widest sections of the valley and each had a generous amount of river frontage. McGregor reported that about half the men moved off their lands while the rest "made a shift to live."

The groups, as well as the blocks, disintegrated. Most of the discharged soldiers had no particular desire to maintain regimental ties or a military chain of command and without strong religious or social bonds, group settlements in New Brunswick and Nova Scotia suffered the fate of group settlements elsewhere; ties and attractions other than, in this case, regimental ones, were much more compelling. In New Brunswick, too, several of the planned groups never formed. When they arrived in Saint John, soldiers from the Loyalist regiments found that while they had been garrisoning New York, civilians—whom they had helped to evacuate—had taken up the lands along the tributaries and lakes in the lower parts of the valley. Five of the regiments who had drawn blocks above present-day Woodstock (150 miles upriver from Saint John) refused to occupy them even when, following their initial refusal, they were offered lots with unusually wide frontages: 42 rods (693 feet) for privates and NCOs and 82 rods (1,353 feet) for officers. Even accessible lots were spurned; in some of the blocks nearer Fredericton, fewer than one man in ten went to his assigned land. When regimental blocks came up for regranting at the turn of the century, only 5 to 6 percent of the regiments could be found on their assigned blocks.

Along the St Croix and in the Passamaquoddy region, the few scattered soldier settlements were even less successful. In November 1783 Peter Clinch of the Royal Fencible Americans had command of a party of soldiers who were landed, as his son described the incident later, in a "howling wilderness" at the mouth of the Magaguadavic River. They had been assigned land on the L'Etang peninsula. The captain of the vessel was so afraid that the soldiers would not stay ashore that he sailed away the moment he got them landed. That night, Peter Clinch slept in the open air under such heavy snowfall that in the morning he had some difficulty removing his blankets. He expected little of the "old soldiers." While provisions lasted, not much land was cleared, the men loitering in places where rum was to be had, making a few shingles, catching fish, and occasionally hunting. In a letter to the provincial secretary in February 1785, Clinch complained of the behaviour of Captain Philip Bailey, the officer in charge of government rations. Instead of issuing tools and proper rations, Bailey gave the soldiers "Rum and Slops," the former becoming, "like the current coin of other countrys...the standard by which they estimated all commodities." Clinch concluded that the majority of the inhabitants of Harbour L'Etang, near present day St. George, are "drunken, dissolute, disbanded soldiers."

In New Brunswick, as in Nova Scotia, the only stable soldier settlements were on rich bottomlands or intervals. Soldiers assigned to the "uplands" quickly gave up the struggle, many taking up General John Graves Simcoe's offer of fertile free land in Ontario. Others fell by the wayside even in areas of good land, the often languid life of soldiering, with its periods of enforced idleness, being no preparation for the rigours of pioneer farming. Married men in remote locations fretted about the education of their children, and young single men, with no reasonable prospect of marriage and family life, could not be kept on their grants. The muster of the Duke of Cumberland's regiment at Chedabucto in June 1784 could raise only nine women, all married, against 149 officers and men. It was, as A.C. Jost remarked, "almost a womanless Eden." The regiment's last official request, made by corpsmen first to a Halifax officer then to the Earl of Manchester, was for English women as wives, homemakers, and helpmates.

A few observers praised the cohesion of some of the former military units but most found only disorder and disarray: "vice of every kind, incident of the camp" and the dominance of "rum and idle habits contracted during the war." One suffering soldier and farmer, "a poor subaltern of an extravagant regimental mess," confided that he had to "hold up, stop [his] grog, and live on pork for at least one muster." To avoid the work of felling and clearing, officers flush with money from the final settlement of their services, and with the prospect of half-pay to come, were only too glad to buy existing farms on which they and their families could settle at once. For a few years they might have been able to sustain the kind of gentlemanly life prized by the Loyalist leaders but eventually most farms were sold or abandoned. Particularly careless, according to Patrick Campbell, were British half-pay officers whom he found lacking in "foresight, industry, [and] prudence." He wrote that when settling their grants, their first concern was to build "a genteel house, in which they could entertain their friends in a becoming stile." In the inevitable interval between the exhaustion of one payment and the arrival of the next, they turned to local merchants for credit and when the debt mounted to unpayable proportions they did a moonlight flit to Great Britain or Ireland, damning the country and declaring that the devil himself could not live in it.

In general, officers from the Loyalist regiments did better than British regulars. Patrick Campbell singled out a Captain French who "by laudable attention and industry...lives in affluence...while many of his brother officers...get in debt, become poor, and the next thing to bankruptcy." But of all the military settlers the most successful, according to Campbell, were the humble footsoldiers: privates and NCO's, toughened by life at the bottom of the military ladder.

Although quite destitute when they took their grants, many, at the time of Campbell's visit, had four to eight cows, access to local markets and, according to Campbell, a life more comfortable than the lives of their officers. On the Nashwaak, Patrick Campbell visited Alexander McIntosh, formerly of the 71st British Regiment. In six years McIntosh and his wife had cleared a "considerable farm" on which they kept cows and hens and grew hay and vegetables. From their maple trees they made sugar and "the finest molasses," ie. syrup, that Campbell had ever tasted." The only shortcoming of the country, in Grace McIntosh's eyes, was that it was not Scotland. They had "every necessary of life in abundance on their...property" but she yearned for her old home, telling Patrick Campbell: "This is an ugly country that has no heather. I never yet saw any good or pleasant place without it."

Black Loyalist Settlements

Even less successful than the attempts to make farmers of soldiers were those aimed at settling former Black slaves in rural communities. In November 1775, in an effort to strengthen the Loyalist forces, John Murray, the Royal Governor of Virginia, promised freedom to "all indented servants [and] negroes" willing to serve as soldiers in British and Loyalist regiments. This was followed, in 1779, by a proclamation from Sir Henry Clinton, the British Commander-in-Chief, offering the same terms to Black slaves willing to serve the regiments in any capacity at all. Tens of thousands responded, marking the largest escape by Blacks in the history of North American slavery. Some 3,500 of them eventually reached Nova Scotia and New Brunswick. Few White Loyalists regarded Blacks as fit recruits but both British and Loyalist American regiments needed tradesmen, labourers, and servants. Black men served as valets, coopers, tailors, blacksmiths, carpenters, and bakers, and Black women as general servants, cooks, and laundresses. Almost every regiment, had Black drummers and buglers, as well as guides to lead them through swamps, woods, and enemy lines. There was, however, only one all-Black regiment, the Black Pioneers, led by white or mixed-race officers.

On disbandment, Blacks were promised land and provisions on the same terms as White Loyalist soldiers, but as former slaves they were expected to become household servants and labourers, not independent farmers. They had no money, no experience of ownership and, with few exceptions, no experience of clearing land and building houses in a wilderness. In Nova Scotia, Governor Parr and his Council made every effort to segregate and scatter them in small communities but eventually most gravitated to the larger towns. Inevitably, they were always last in line for land grants and government provisions; few received any land at all, and these only after the needs of White settlers had been satisfied. At Shelburne, the lands assigned to them, buried for the most part in "deep Swamps" and "impenetrable Woods," were several miles north-west of the town. Of the 649 Black men at Shelburne (about a third of whom were former soldiers) only 184 received farm lots, and these averaged only 34 acres. Others were forced to buy their farms from earnings made in the town, but the majority remained landless.

Elsewhere in Nova Scotia, the story was the same. At Digby, Chedabucto, and Tracadie Harbour the Blacks either received no land at all or their lots were much smaller than those granted to White settlers. At Brindley, near Digby, 70 Pioneers were settled on one-acre plots with the expectation of getting government provisions and land for farms. But the farm lots assigned to them proved, after the first two surveys, to belong to other settlers. Before another survey

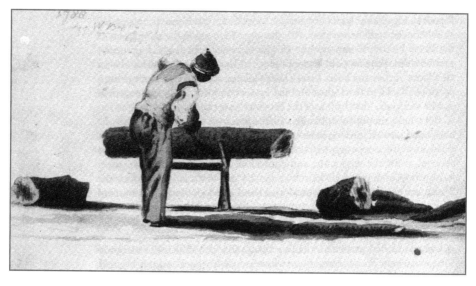

A drawing of a Birchtown workman.

National Archives of Canada

could be undertaken, the government had stopped paying its deputy survey-ors. Not until September 1789 was there a successful survey for the Pioneers but before they could receive title to their lands, in 1801, most of them had left Nova Scotia. In general, Black Loyalists fared no better with provisions. In 1791 John Clarkson, an English abolitionist, reported to William Wilberforce that he could produce innumerable witnesses who had not received even one year's provisions, far less the three they had been promised. He also knew of many

who had "neither received a mouthful of provisions, or so much as an imple-
ment of husbandry." The Digby Blacks received rations for only a few months
and for these they were forced to work on the township's roads, a condition not
required of disbanded White soldiers.

In Saint John, a number of free Blacks were offered small town lots and,
attracted by government food and provisions, these and others stayed in the
city. In 1785 Governor Carleton suggested that free Blacks interested in rural
land should form themselves
into companies and that each
company be given a block of
land near the city. Initially,
each settler would receive fifty
acres with the promise of more
if he proved capable of
improving them. By 1785,
however, all the good land
along the Saint John and its
tributaries had already been
granted in 100- to 1,000-acre
lots. All that remained for the
Blacks were leftover areas
between existing grants. In
June 1785 George Sproule
received a warrant from
Governor Carleton to divide
land in the lower valley into
50-acre lots, designated for the
"accommodation of a number
of Black persons." On one side
of the block was a lieutenant
and on the other disbanded
men from British regiments.
The grant also seems to have

*Drum of the New Jersey Volunteers, 2nd
Battalion, 1777.*

New Brunswick Museum

been too small for the purpose, George Sproule having to instruct deputy surveyor Thomas Harper that if there was not enough river frontage in the designated area then he was to survey lots in the rear of the lots for the disbanded
men. A month later, in July 1785, Sproule instructed Richard Holland to subdi-
vide nine lots of 200 acres between the Kennebecasis and the Long Reach of the
Saint John River into 50-acre lots for a group of Blacks. The interfluve land

between the Kennebecasis and the Long Reach is some of the roughest on the Kingston Peninsula.

Black frustrations were so deep that by 1791 more than 1,000 Black Loyalists had petitioned the Nova Scotia government for permission to emigrate to Sierra Leone. Their objective was to join, at the bidding of the remarkable Thomas Peters, the remnant of a self-governing colony of free Blacks established by English abolitionists on the west coast of Africa. As well as offering a more hospitable social and political climate, Peters concluded that the physical climate of Sierra Leone might also be more accommodating to black Loyalists. After six years of fruitless petitioning in Fredericton and Halifax on behalf of the Blacks, Peters, a former plantation slave from North Carolina and a sergeant in the Black Pioneers, had gone to London to lay the grievances of Nova Scotia's Blacks before the imperial government. In London he met William Wilberforce and Granville Sharp who were then looking for ways to revitalize the Anti-Slavery Society's struggling West African colony. Poor planning, a difficult environment, and the hostility of local tribes had brought the colony to its knees. In October 1791 an agent of the Sierra Leone Company arrived in Halifax and travelled widely throughout the province meeting groups of Black settlers. In return for a modest quitrent, or property tax, the Company promised each freedman twenty acres for himself, ten for his wife, and five for each child. It also promised protection from marauding slave traders. A year later, in January 1792, a fleet carrying 1,190 Blacks—222 from New Brunswick—left Halifax for Africa.

The Parish and the County

Although the world of large estates, small yeomen, and tenant farms envisaged by the Loyalist leaders never materialized, the dream of a society governed by a privileged class of gentlemen farmers and landowners was given up only reluctantly. On taking office in New Brunswick, Governor Thomas Carleton declared in a letter to Lord Sydney that during his administration there would be no undermining of the central authority: no nursing, as he put it, of "the American spirit of innovation" among "the Loyal Refugee." In a breathtaking understatement he announced his intention of making a "small deviation," from the constitution of Nova Scotia where everything originated, according to New England, with the Assembly. To limit the power of an elected assembly, he meant to have his executive and key officials in place before one could be convened. With the exception of one very successful merchant, William Hazen, his 12-member Council was made up entirely of lawyers and large landowners.

His most singular tactic in the drive toward oligarchy, however, was to make the parish, with its associations of obedience and pastoral order, the unit of local government and to make it completely subservient to the county. He was particularly anxious to avoid town meetings, which he and the New England Loyalists regarded as seedbeds of disaffection in the former American colonies. In the lower and middle reaches of the Saint John Valley, which had been divided into townships on the arrival of the Saint John Society in 1765, this meant re-drawing the administrative map. As if to underline his intentions he divided Maugerville, the largest pre-Loyalist community in the province, into two parishes. These, like all the other parishes, were to depend on the central government for funds and on county officials for direction and control.

As in England, the county was to be a conduit for royal and parliamentary power. Carleton's county magistrates, who were appointed by the Governor and Council, were expected to emulate English justices of the peace. The latter were unpaid and drawn invariably from the ranks of the gentry. Carleton's magistrates, too, represented the "best gentlemen" available, but as pioneer landowners and merchants of limited means, few managed to remain neutral, using the office as an avenue to government positions. The sharp-tongued Bishop Inglis likened them to the most marginal of the English justices: "trading justices" or justices of "mean degree." Until replaced by elected councils in the 1850s, New Brunswick's county magistrates ran the parishes, levying taxes, overseeing law enforcement, licensing teachers and taverns, appointing trustees to the parish schools, controlling public lands, and filling the offices of minor officialdom: constables, fence viewers, pound keepers, surveyors of fish and lumber, hogreeves, and assessors.

As if to reinforce the image of the county as a functional rather than a nominal division, New Brunswick's counties, as Esther Clark Wright pointed out, are recognizable geographical entities. Definition of the county boundaries rested on the perception, so often ignored by bureaucrats, that rivers unite populations rather than divide them. In southern New Brunswick it was the watersheds or interfluves, not the streams themselves, that separated the counties. Along the lower Saint John the parallel troughs of the Kennebecasis and the Long Reach-Belleisle Bay became King's County; those of the Washdemoak and Grand Lake, Queen's County. Saint John County encompasses both the mouth of the river, the city, and the coastal strips on each side. In the upper valley, the regimental lands above Fredericton and the uncharted areas beyond became York County. West of Saint John, the Passamaquoddy region and the St. Croix formed the heart of Charlotte County and, to the east, the Tantramar marshes and the Petitcodiac and Memramcook Rivers the heart of Westmoreland County.

Naming New Brunswick's counties might have been an arbitrary procedure but there was nothing arbitrary about their delineation. Today they frame communities and, to the surprise of visitors to whom counties are nothing more than an administrative convenience, they serve as vital points of reference.

With its large contingent of republican-leaning New Englanders, Nova Scotia, unlike New Brunswick, was unreceptive ground for an oligarchy of landlords and a top-heavy system of counties and parishes. As an inducement to

General Thomas Carleton, governor of New Brunswick 1784-86; lieutenant-governor, 1786-1817.

University of New Brunswick

settle in the province, the New England Planters had been promised the same religious and civic freedoms that they had enjoyed in Massachusetts, Connecticut, and Rhode Island. The most fundamental of civic freedoms, and the one from which all others flowed, was the power to allocate land. In New England, land was granted not in small lots to individuals but in large units—plantations or townships—to groups of settlers. Within the townships land was allocated and local affairs supervised by a township committee. Government in eighteenth-century New England meant local government and, as Michael Zuckermann has suggested, it scarcely mattered if the central government was in Boston or London. Power was the power of neighbours agreeing or disagreeing at the village hall or tavern, not something that descended mysteriously from above. But with local power came local responsibility: for the care of the poor, the maintenance of the roads, peace-keeping, and the support of schools the township had to fend for itself.

In keeping with New England practice, Nova Scotia allocated roughly 12-

mile-square blocks of 100,000 acres to each of the township associations. Provincial surveyors, who in pre-Loyalist days seem to have been mostly retired seamen using marine compasses, codlines, and marine terminology, surveyed the perimeter of the block but left the demarcation and distribution of town and farm lots to the grantees. On arrival at Annapolis, in May 1760, 31 men brought from Boston in the *Charming Molly* convened, in what was the first township meeting in Nova Scotia, to appoint lot layers and other township officials. Most of the wives, women, and children had been left behind until living quarters could be readied.

The nature and disposition of the lots varied from township to township but in all cases the guiding principle was to give each grantee some of the good land. At Annapolis, for example, each got a portion of the lowland formerly cultivated by the Acadians and each a portion—much larger—of the upland. The objective was to give all settlers an equal start and by scattering the parcels of land encourage nucleated, European-style village settlement. For a small family, the usual land allotment was about 500 acres or one share. For large families and single people the allotments were 750 acres and 250 acres respectively. To discourage speculation and the growth of a landlord or rentier class, no one grant was to exceed 1,000 acres.

Jonathan Belcher, Chief Justice of Nova Scotia.

Private Collection

But the attempt to create compact villages proved fruitless, the grantees from the outset buying, selling, and exchanging lots to make consolidated holdings on which they built their houses.

The townships themselves also proved to be unstable. No sooner had the surveyors finished their work than the Nova Scotia counties launched their attack upon them. In New England, where the townships had preceded both state and county organizations, the counties were weak or non existent. But in Nova Scotia five county boundaries had been drawn in 1759, a year before the arrival of the New Englanders. Governor Lawrence's proclamations of 1758-59 had promised each township considerable powers of autonomy but from the outset the townships lay in the shadow of the counties. In 1760 Governor Lawrence died suddenly and his successor, Chief Justice Belcher, was much less sympathetic to the Planters. He promptly repealed the act (of 1760) that allowed each township to apportion its land, and he replaced the township committees with appointees of the Governor and Council. The Planters protested Belcher's "uncommon and tyrannical conduct" but despite strong backing from Charles Morris and Richard Bulkeley, Secretary to the Council, the townships were never incorporated.

In 1763, a Council bill empowering the townships to elect town officers, mend their streets and highways, and maintain their poor was thoroughly emasculated by the Assembly. At the end of the session, maintenance of the poor was the only autonomy left to the townships. As D.C. Harvey remarked, there were to be no 20 little republics in Nova Scotia. For a time, the more distant townships enjoyed some measure of the Yankee system of local control but their powers were slowly undermined as the county magistrates, who were directly responsible to the Governor, assumed the functions of the township committees. To add insult to injury, the New Englanders often found themselves assigned to poundkeeping, fenceminding, and peacekeeping—the least attractive of the parish jobs. The emasculation of the townships led to protests in Liverpool in 1762 and in King's County in 1765, and it may well have fuelled sympathy for the Revolution.

Chapter Two

Building the Towns

T he failure of the estates and military settlements, and the marginal nature of farming except on rich valley and bottomland soils, were hammer blows to the dream of a society of obedient farmers governed by a land-owning elite. Winslow attributed the general weakness of farming, and the decline of farming communities, to the absence of a clearly defined chain of authority and the fecklessness of many of the individual settlers, who, once the government bounty was exhausted, sold their lands for a trifle to land jobbers and speculators. The real culprits, however, were not individual or societal weaknesses but the Maritime climate and Maritime soils. Clearing the land simply did not make it fertile. Winslow, who was as committed as anyone to the dream of an agricultural society, was dismayed by the general reversal of fortunes wrought by the frontier. Officers and gentlemen tied to unprofitable farms were reduced to a life of drudgery while shoemakers, he wrote despondently, "have all turned merchants and appear to have made their fortunes." Although the population remained heavily rural, social and political power shifted inexorably in the direction of commerce and trade: "Our gentlemen," Winslow wrote in 1793, "have all become potato-planters, and our shoemakers [turned merchants] are preparing to legislate." The Loyalist dream had turned on itself.

To limit the power of Saint John and promote the image of an agrarian society, Winslow campaigned to locate the provincial capital in the middle reaches of the Saint John Valley where the land was, as he put it, "inconceivably fertile." Winslow's aim was to draw settlement inland away from Saint John and the coast, and, by doing so, mollify the Loyalist regiments who resented their relegation to the upper and less accessible reaches of the valley. In the fall of 1783 some 2,000 of them had been taken in boatloads 75 miles upstream to St. Ann's Point, formerly the site of a Maliseet summer camp and a short-lived Acadian village destroyed by a British force in 1759. The obvious site for an inland capital was the established Planter settlement at Maugerville but the Planters, from Essex County, Massachusetts, were openly republican and their village flood-prone. St. Ann's Point, on the other hand, was elevated, politically untainted, and located just below the river's first rapids and shallows, at the head of navigation for all vessels larger than a sloop.

View of Halifax from Fort Needham in 1781.

National Archives of Canada

Needing a town, the regiments began to lay one out only to have their work halted two months later by the partition of Nova Scotia and the choice of St. Ann's Point as the site for the capital of the new province, the "Metropolis of New Brunswick." Unlike Winslow and other Loyalist leaders, when making his decision Governor Carleton was probably influenced as much by military considerations as a distrust of cities and commerce. In addition to promoting agriculture, a capital in the middle reaches of the valley would be an effective link in land communications between Halifax and Quebec City. The governor's choice of Fredericton undoubtedly pleased the regiments, but the merchants of Saint John were justifiably incensed. It was as clear to them, as it had been to James Peters, that the Loyalist "capital" should be the port settlement that commanded the mouth of the Saint John River and, *ipso facto*, the trade and commerce of the country lying along its banks.

However strong their distrust of commercial towns and cities, the Loyalist leaders were powerless to prevent their growth. Towns were needed to service the rural population and, in any case, many of the refugees were merchants and tradesmen, not farmers and fishermen. New towns were built at the mouths of rivers, at the heads of harbours and bays, and in productive sections of the valleys. In the settled parts of peninsular Nova Scotia, Loyalists also moved into existing towns. Populations doubled and even quadrupled overnight, inciting the wrath of the earlier residents who made the newcomers pay dearly for their inconvenience. Annapolis prices, for example, were said to be higher than New York's. Halifax, a town of barely 2,000 in 1782, took in several thousand refugees. In October 1782, Annapolis Royal grew from roughly 120 to more than 600. Hundreds more arrived in November causing an increase so sudden that Jacob Bailey, the Anglican missionary, was unable to make "a proper computation."

Plans and Surveys

Laying out towns in the British colonies was a matter of following instructions issued by the Board of Trade and Plantations, an advisory commission appointed by the king. The instructions, in the form of a series of directives rather than actual plans, advised field surveyors where to locate a town, how to fortify it, how to ensure a food supply, and how to lay out the streets and squares. As in all planning exercises requiring speed and simplicity, geometry ruled. British colonial towns, like Greek and Roman ones, were to be regular patterns of straight streets and rectangular blocks. Ideally, each town had a main square, in the centre of the plan if the town was inland and in the centre of the waterfront if on a shore. Subsidiary squares were reserved for courthouses, hospitals, and schools, and on the edge of the town land was set aside for fortifications, barracks, and commons. Orientation, where possible, was to be southerly. Idiosyncracies of terrain and the freedom granted surveyors meant that royal instructions were seldom followed to the letter, but the pattern of open squares and straight streets crossing at right angles generally prevailed.

Right-angled plans were easy to survey and the lots, being rectangular, were easy to describe and allocate. But although expedient, town plans of unwavering regularity also reflected the temper of the times. The rediscovery of classical form in France and England, and Newton's conception of a mechanical universe subject to immutable mathematical laws, called for symmetry and balance in architecture and town planning. The object of both was to create an earthly order in harmony with the demonstrated cosmic one. The ideal Georgian

(English Renaissance) town plan was a harmonious arrangement of circles or squares connected by a balanced network of streets. British exemplars of the genre were Edinburgh New Town, Bath, and the residential extensions to eighteenth-century London.

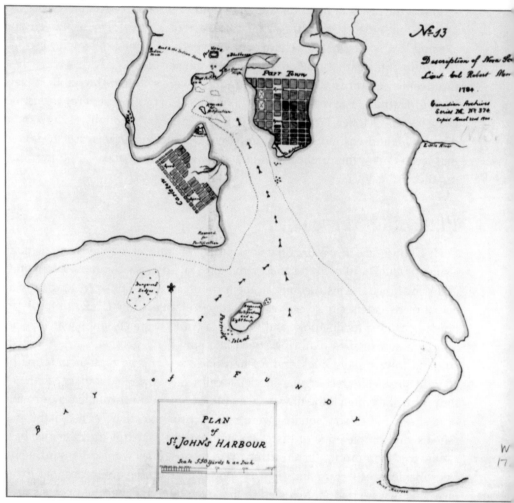

Map of Saint John and its harbour, 1784 (G. William Lambton).

New Brunswick Museum

But notions of classical symmetry and Newtonian order were hardly the preoccupations of colonial surveyors. With government instructions in one hand and a level in the other, they quickly laid out a pattern of straight streets and rectangular blocks interrupted by open squares. Patterned towns of this kind extended in a broad arc from the Southern and Middle Colonies through New

England to Prince Edward Island and Nova Scotia. Halifax, Lunenburg, Charlottetown, and the New England Planter towns all had regular, rectilinear plans. The larger towns were wide and deep but the smaller ones were mere tracings: often just a few parallel streets crossed by lanes running down to the river or the shore. Gagetown on the Saint John River, for example, is a town of four streets running parallel to the river and three full and two partial intersecting streets running down to the water.

For the most part, town planning in the colonies was a routine exercise that called for judgement rather than imagination. The surveyor's function was to devise a workable marriage between the Board of Trade's guidelines and the idiosyncrasies of the site. Invention and imagination came into play only when the surveyor or planner had the authority or the confidence to ignore the directions of the Board.

The only true independent in the Maritimes was J.F.W. DesBarres, governor of the then separate province of Cape Breton and an accomplished

J.F.W. DesBarres, Governor of Cape Breton 1784-87.

Private Collection

Woolwich Academy-trained cartographer. As the site for his capital DesBarres chose not the French fortress at Louisbourg but a mining settlement on a peninsula at the head of the south arm of the Spanish River. With a touching disregard for embellishment, DesBarres named the capital Coal Mines but within a year protocol triumphed, the name being changed to honour Lord Sydney, the British Secretary of State. DesBarres's 1786 plan for Sydney was an intricate pattern of residential crescents and squares linked by axial streets. He reserved a central square for a government house and offices, and a Grand Circus in the style of the one at Bath for the most prestigious houses. The circus also featured an octagonally shaped church. At distances of between four and seven miles south and east of the main town he laid out five satellite communities, each circular, organized around a central plaza and linked to Sydney by boulevards. Properties along the boulevards increased in size with distance from the town centres.

Swiss- or French-born DesBarres might have been familiar with the principles of Renaissance town planning but he was no judge of the potential of Cape
Breton. Only about 400 Loyalists were attracted to the island, and they were
soon at odds with the governor. Desbarres granted title to lands only when he
was compelled to do so and government supplies were irregular and often so
inadequate that, from time to time, the Loyalists were thrown onto the governor's bounty. Not surprisingly, Sydney failed to live up to Desbarres's expectations. An early visitor described it as a dismal town of "about 50 hovels,"
lacking even the "smallest trace of industry as the inhabitants live by selling
rum to the soldiers."

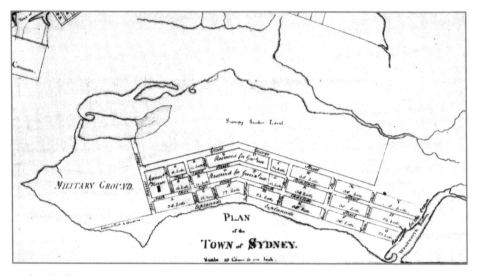

*A detail of a plan of Sydney drafted by an anonymous source—this plan, unlike
most town plans of the era, followed the angle of the shoreline.*

In the old province of Nova Scotia, town surveys were the responsibility of
the surveyor-general, Charles Morris. If done in advance of settlement, the procedure was straightforward. In St. Andrews, for example, the surveyors arrived
in the middle of August, 1784, and by the end of September they had surveyed
the streets and house lots and divided much of the adjacent shore and river land
into 100-acre farm or "garden" lots. The town plat, a half-mile deep and one mile
wide, was a text book example of a colonial plan. The streets were broad and
straight and the main square, as prescribed for coastal towns, was in the middle
of the street closest to the shore. The only departures from strict symmetry
were the narrow waterfront lots, of unequal lengths because the shore was not
a straight line. If allowance is made for differences in scale, the St. Andrews

plan is much like William Penn's 1682 plan for Philadelphia, while Penn's plan might well have been inspired by Richard Newcourt's plan (never implemented) for the rebuilding of London after the Great Fire of 1666. In the mid 1660s Penn studied law at London's Inns of Court.

As the last of the major Loyalist settlements in the Maritimes, St. Andrews had all the advantages of hindsight. Scouts sent out from the mother town of Castine, Maine, chose a gently sloping, south-facing site on a peninsula in a bay at the mouth of a river—the St. Croix. The situation offered not only clear prospects for trade and agriculture but it duplicated conditions at Castine. Settlers bound for the new town, who had gathered in Castine, drew lots before

"Drawing Lots."

C. W. Jefferys, Imperial Oil Collection

embarkation. One of them, Nathaniel Palmer, mentions being present at "a general drawing for Town Lotts by the settlers for the New Town of St. Andrews." As in the New England townships, each adult settler, or head of family, was entitled to a town lot and a "garden" lot, in this case of 100 acres, outside the town. But as a settlement of merchants most were uninterested in farmland, 80 percent of the 430 original grants consisting of a town lot only. On arrival, the Loyalists were met by officers of the Penobscot Association who directed them to their lots, each town lot being described by division, lot number, and letter.

A sketch of St. Andrews, 1840, by Frederick Wells of the 1st Royals. In the foreground recently cleared farm lots run down to the St. Croix River.

New Brunswick Museum

For late arrivals and industrious squatters, magistrates had the power to allocate lots not yet taken up and when more land was needed they applied to Halifax for a 20-rod extension along the entire back of the town. Even though the most prominent Loyalists managed to acquire the most sought after town sites and garden lots, in St. Andrews there seems to have been very little squabbling over property.

Other settlements, however, were not as fortunate. With refugees crowding into the British-held ports, town sites were chosen quickly and often unwisely.

Uppermost in the minds of the Loyalist scouts and agents was the need to maintain commercial and political links with Great Britain and the West Indies. The chief, and in many cases only, priority was a good harbour, the choice often being made in complete ignorance of the character of the interior. "Very few people," Thomas Pynchon noted, "[have] any further acquaintance with the land than the heads of the harbours." Two cases in point were the towns of Port Mouton (formerly Guysborough), on Nova Scotia's south shore and Bellevue (now Beaver Harbour) on the east side of New Brunswick's Passamaquoddy Bay. The Bellevue settlers were Quakers from Pennsylvania and New Jersey who, harassed for their neutrality during the war, sailed from New York in the late summer of 1783. Guided by their agents, they moved thirty miles down the coast from Saint John to a neatly gridded townsite beside a rockbound harbour. To the north of the townsite were smallholdings of a few acres each and to the west ten acre plots intended for Anabaptists who never came. By 1786 the colony was said to have had between two and three hundred houses and a population of about 800. None, by dint of a declaration from the founders of the settlement, were slaves. Although the harbour was excellent the colony produced no surpluses for trade and, the land being unfarmable, it was forced to subsist on government rations and shipments of materials and food from Quaker societies in England and America. In 1790 a forest fire swept through the near-defunct town and most of the few remaining settlers moved a few miles inland to a farmable plateau which they named Pennfield Ridge. A census of the parish of Pennfield in 1803 reported 54 inhabitants.

Port Mouton, so Thomas Raddall suspected, was probably conceived over an inaccurate map in the gunroom or "great cabin" of H.M.S. *Cyclops*, anchored in Shelburne Harbour. The surveyor, William Morris, was asked to lay out a township in the New England fashion: a rectangle with a four-mile frontage on the bay and extending ten miles inland. The plan for the townsite is presumed to have been based on the nearby Planter town of Liverpool where Morris spent two days before beginning his survey. At Port Mouton he laid out shore lots for wharves and warehouses and above these he placed the town itself: three streets half a mile long paralleling the shore, crossed by three lanes running down to the water. Behind the town he laid off a rectangular common, and on the southwest side a number of "sea-lots" to be used for drying fish. The town was named Guysborough in honour of Sir Guy Carleton. Inland, along the river, Morris marked out 100-acre strips, each bearing the name of the grantee. On paper, Raddall noted, the plan looked perfect and no doubt pleased the surveyor-general in Halifax. In practice, however, the scheme was a catastrophe that, like Bellevue, was spared a lingering death by a disastrous fire the following spring. A few of the 2,400 settlers hung on but most departed, some for Morristown (now St. Stephen) at the head of navigation (the fishing falls) on the St. Croix and some for Chedabucto Bay where a new Guysborough would eventually emerge from, metaphorically speaking, the ashes of the old.

If St. Andrews was a model town settlement then its alter ego was Port Roseway (now Shelburne) at the mouth of the Roseway River on the southwest shore of Nova Scotia. Whereas St. Andrews brought up the rear of settlement, and had the advantage of hindsight, Shelburne was in the vanguard. Few towns have had such buoyant beginnings. With its magnificent harbour, the "best landfall in the province [for] all European vessels," Shelburne was to be the Loyalists' crowning achievement: "the most flourishing town for trade in any part of the world." To lay out the townsite and the adjacent country lots, the surveyor-general, William Morris, engaged Benjamin Marston, one of 23 deputy surveyors hired that spring. Marston, a former merchant and shipowner with no formal training in surveying, and no practical experience of it, owed his appointment to the patronage of his cousin Edward Winslow. In his approach to Winslow, Marston had not asked to be a surveyor even though it is likely that he had picked up the principles of surveying at Harvard. But as well as being well-connected, in a world where connections meant everything, Marston had ability. He proved to be a capable, if irascible, practitioner. He was also an inventive one, patenting a sextant (a variation of Hadley's Quadrant) that could measure the sun's altitude when the horizon was invisible.

In Halifax, Charles Morris's instructions to Marston were to proceed to Port Roseway and there to lay out a town "agreeable to the design already approved for that purpose." Anticipating an initial embarkation of 3,000 (all members of the Port Roseway Associates of New York) compared with 15,000 for St. Andrews, Governor Parr set aside four townships each of 100,000 acres. The town plan, drawn up in Halifax and approved by Governor Parr and Sir Guy Carleton in New York, consisted of five parallel streets intersected by cross streets, arranged around a large square. The land between the front street and the shore was laid out in lanes and small allotments so that each of the Port Roseway Associates might get a town lot and a water lot. In practice, however, water lots were reserved for those associates needing places for workshops, stores, warehouses, and wharves.

Accompanied by William Morris, the son of the surveyor-general, Marston sailed from Halifax, picked up a set of surveying instruments at Lunenburg, and arrived in Port Roseway on 2 May, 1783. He and Morris spent the day following their arrival exploring the country and choosing a townsite. The following day

A sketch of St Andrews in the 1850s (Lieutenant Clarke's New Brunswick sketches, 1853-1857.

National Archives of Canada

thirty vessels of the "spring" fleet sailed into Shelburne harbour, delivering 3,000 Loyalists. Among them were more than 900 former slaves. In the interests of orderly settlement, the Port Roseway Associates had, on the recommendation of Sir Guy Carleton, divided themselves into 16 militia companies, with each company led by a captain, two lieutenants and four sergeants. The captains, commissioned by Sir Guy, were to serve as interim magistrates until the government of Nova Scotia could appoint permanent ones.

On arrival at Port Roseway, the evacuees promptly rejected the townsite chosen by Marston and Morris and to choose another they appointed three men from each of the 16 companies. To Marston, an arch Tory, government by representative committee seemed only one remove from mob rule: "This cursed republican, town meeting spirit," he confided to his diary, "has been the ruin of us already....Mankind oftentimes [possesses] too much liberty." William Morris, too, was upset by the dissension, finding none of that lofty unanimity and disinterestedness he had expected in a people professing such high ideals. After more bickering, a new townsite was chosen on what many still considered "a rough, uneven piece of land," and on May 9, 1783, Morris and Marston were able to lay out the centre street of the town: King Street, running back from the shore.

The beginning of the survey was a signal for cooperative action, however brief. To lighten the work of the surveyors, people began, Marston recorded, "very cheerfully to cut down the trees." But it was, he added ominously, "a new employment to many of them." On the following day he and Morris marked the line for Water Street and surveyed two blocks on each side of King Street. Although waterfront lots for warehouses and wharves were not part of the original plan, they marked out a few blocks of narrow lots running, as in St. Andrews, from Water Street down to the shore. Ideally, each settler would have a warehouse lot and a town lot and, outside the town, a 50-acre farm lot.

For four days the Shelburne Loyalists laboured, cutting trees, slashing underbrush, and generally assisting the surveyors. On the fifth day they grew tired, or bored, some not coming to work until eleven in the morning and some not coming at all. Soon the flow became a trickle and on some days it stopped altogether: "From 1/2 past 5 to 8," reads one irritable entry in Marston's diary, "and not a soul in town to assist me."

With few Loyalists willing to work, Marston and Morris had to call on Royal Engineers for help with the surveying and on British naval ratings for cutting trees and clearing brush. Marston noted in his journal that city life and the easy pickings of war had left many of the Loyalists unfit for toil. "Barbers, Taylors, Shoemakers, and all kinds of mechanics, bred and used to live in great towns," he wrote sternly, "are inured to habits very unfit for undertakings which require hardiness, resolution, industry and patience." The lack of country conditioning and the general conviction that Britain, having failed them at the peace table, now owed them a living, brought on a perplexing lassitude. After his visit in the summer of 1783 Governor Parr reported that some of the Loyalists demanded "exorbitant pay" even for helping with the chaining of their own lands. In a letter to Amos Botsford, written in July 1783, the Provincial Secretary Richard Bulkeley also marvelled at their dependence,

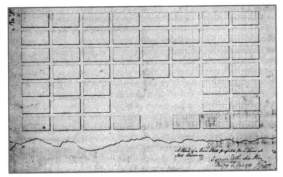

Plan of Port Roseway (Shelburne) signed and approved by Governor Parr, 1783.

Nova Scotia Department of Natural Recourses

Shelburne from the barracks on the west side of the harbour (Lieutenant H. Pooley, c. 1820).

William Inglis Morse Collection, Special Collections, Dalhousie University Libraries.

wondering how 10,000 people could have come to settle lands in Nova Scotia without one set of survey instruments among them.

Attracted by its accessibility from New York and possibly by the name "Roseway," refugees and disbanded soldiers from both provincial and British regiments continued to pour into Shelburne during the summer and fall of 1783. The "fall" fleet left New York in the middle of September, and shiploads of refugees continued to arrive until the final evacuation of the city in late November. By the end of the year, Shelburne's population had more than doubled, to roughly 8,500. Unable to keep up with the demand for both town and farm lots, Marston and his three assistant surveyors—Morris having left to survey other Loyalist settlements—were quickly reduced to surveying blocks, leaving the delineation and allocation of the individual lots to the civilian associations and the Loyalist corps.

British ships bound for Nova Scotia during the evacuation of New York.

Library of Congress

Yet, in spite of the mounting demand for lots, appeals for help with the chaining and measuring continued to fall on deaf ears. Few Loyalists felt any compunction to help with the survey unless paid to do so. So general was the problem that in 1785 the government was reduced to threatening settlers with the loss of their lots to more cooperative refugees unless they volunteered to work as axe and chain men. In Shelburne, they responded by complaining about the inconvenient location of the only land left for town lots and pressed instead for the subdivision into house lots of the open squares reserved as settings for public buildings. Predictably, Marston attributed their indiscipline to lack of leadership; the captains of the militia groups being of the same class as most of the refugees, were unused to command. The leaderless mob, "sheep without a shepherd," made his life a misery. "Dinned to death for Town lots and Water lots, for 50 acre and 500-acre lots ," he wrote distractedly to Edward Winslow, " my head is so full of Triangles, Squares, Parallelograms, Trapezias & Rhomboises that the corners do sometimes almost put my eyes out."

As trying for Marston as the actual surveying was the business of distributing the lots. Town lots were allocated by lottery, a procedure that, as practised in Shelburne, not only tested Loyalist unanimity but strained Marston's patience. "'Tis a task," he wrote, "trying to humanity," and one not made easier by the demand of the Port Roseway associates that they alone should get land.

Tickets for the lottery were made by writing the lot numbers on sheets of paper and carefully twisting the sheets into a roll. As each applicant drew a roll, the number of the lot and the name of the applicant were recorded by Marston in a book of locations. Had the number of lots always equalled or exceeded the number of applicants the procedure would have been straightforward, but in Shelburne the surveyors could never keep up with demand, the number of applicants always exceeding the number of available lots. To prevent rancour, the selection of applicants for the draw would have had to be scrupulously fair but many of the captains of the Loyalist associations had, as Marston put it, "private views." Favouritism was rife and such was

Richard Bulkeley, Provincial Secretary of Nova Scotia.

Public Archives of Nova Scotia

the demand for lots that some were sold immediately after the draw. "Real authority," Marston wrote judiciously, "can never be supported without some degree of real superiority."

In spite of the pressures, Marston was immune to bribery. On August 9, 1783, he noted: "A Capt. McLean has this evening sent a green turtle...he is to have a house lot, but this will not blind my eyes, he must have the same chance as his neighbours who have no turtle to send." As well as protecting the interests of settlers without gifts to offer, Marston also defended Shelburne's Blacks. He dismissed accusations that Black settlers had encroached on White property as a "piece of villainy" and took steps to prevent them from being dispossessed of their lands. His stance made him a target for both refugee and official frustrations. During a riot instigated by disbanded White soldiers, who accused the Blacks of undercutting them in the labour market, Marston's life was threatened. He was forced to take refuge in the Shelburne barracks and from there he made his way to Halifax. He never returned to Shelburne.

In Saint John, as in Shelburne, there was no interval between survey and settlement. No surveyors had been sent ahead of the refugees, three thousand of whom arrived in the Spring fleet of 20 vessels that sailed from New York in late April 1783. The season was late and on the fleet's arrival in the middle of May the ground was still snow-covered. A fall fleet delivered 1,200 more and still others came in individual vessels. Estimates vary but it seems likely that at least five thousand wintered on the two peninsulas that would eventually accommodate the city of Saint. John.

There are no details of the survey but it, too, must have been a task trying to humanity. The surveyor, Paul Bedell, seems to have arrived with the Spring fleet and did not begin the survey until late May or early June. Peter Huggeford, a physician from New York, recorded that he arrived in July, 1783, "whilst the town was still surveying and before any buildings were erected." Both peninsulas were rough masses of rock covered with thick growths of scrub pine and cedar, which had to be cut before even tents could be put up. The trees were cut, but so crudely that the protruding stumps bruised and even broke the ankles of unguarded pedestrians. At night few ventured abroad. Both refugees and provincials put up tents or built temporary huts in the few flats and clearings but because there were no regular streets or lanes only by chance could anyone be found. Like ministering angels, Paul Bedell and his assistants brought order to chaos by laying a grid of streets and squares over the two peninsulas: Parrtown on the east and Carleton on the west. In neither case did Bedell make concessions to slope, the cross streets running uphill against a contour that two centuries of levelling and filling have failed to alleviate. Huge outcrops of rock and a belt of woodland divided Parrtown into two separate areas, Lower Cove and Upper Cove, the only passage between the two being a beach at low tide and a rough track along the high ground.

As in Shelburne, distributing land and government provisions proved stressful. Refugees and provincials arrived in far greater numbers than had been expected and because of delays in the escheating of river valley lands many prospective farmers were forced to put up in the city. Hoping for increases in land values, the holders of unimproved grants in the old townships contested the escheats, blocking access to large sections of the valley. But not even available lands could be settled quickly, surveyors being in such short supply that

Saint John in 1815. Subsumed by the Loyalist ideal, the new, raw seaport has the look of a long-established market town (Joseph Brown Comingo).

New Brunswick Museum

disbanding engineers off arriving vessels had to be dragooned into service. With arrivals equalling or even outnumbering departures, Saint John's population mushroomed, placing ever greater pressure on town lands. Lots were drawn for as they became available, but because there were always more applicants than lots, the lots were divided and subdivided producing, in some cases, parcels one-sixteenth the size of the original.

In a society in which office-seeking and influence-peddling were endemic, favouritism was bound to be an issue. Not even a lottery could prevent many of the choice commercial locations from going to Loyalist agents and their associates. In Parrtown the choice lots were in Upper Cove alongside the sheltered water of Market Slip, the loading and unloading point for the river boats and the heart of the modern city. Among the more prominent recipients was the Reverend John Sayre, who had also managed to have a house built at public expense before he arrived. Sayre, an agent for the Loyalists and a leader of the Committee of Fifty-five, contended that the favour was a fair exchange for service. Yet his confidence that the people "in consideration of our labour as agents...will not object to our having an exclusive choice of lands," proved unfounded. The rank-and-file Loyalists were no more tolerant of privilege in Parrtown than they had been in New York; bitter complaints from the businessmen and disbanded soldiers of Lower Cove led to an official investigation and some redistribution of the prime lots in 1784. But the resentment, which the inquiry had failed to dispel, carried over into the election of 1785 when the "rabble"—as they were dubbed by the official class—of Lower Cove pitted their candidates for the Legislative Assembly against the handpicked candidates of the governor and his council.

The Lower Cove candidates won all six of the available seats by a comfortable margin of 100 votes out of 1,100 votes cast. But an accusation of "shameful and corrupt practices" by powerful residents of Upper Cove forced their withdrawal. The Lower Covers disdained to defend themselves against the charges, whereupon the Sheriff, after an unsupervised scrutiny of the polls, disqualified 200 of their votes to grant the election to the Upper Cove candidates. Selected members of the "rabble" were arrested, charged with criminal activity before the Supreme Court, and punished. Thereafter any resistance to patrician authority in New Brunswick was likely to be dubbed the "Lower Cove stile."

Except that it was rich interval land, St. Ann's plain, unlike Saint John's two rocky peninsulas, was an ideal site for a city. It was in the centre of a potentially rich agricultural district, at the head of navigation of the Saint John and if not quite, as Winslow put it, "exalted above all Freshets," it was safe from most of them. As if responding to the generous nature of the site, Charles Morris instructed that the town should be laid out "in the best manner the ground will admit: "streets were to be at least sixty feet wide and at right angles, and there were to be squares or sites as "nearly Central as may be" for public buildings.

To conduct an official survey for the capital, Governor Carleton commissioned Dugald Campbell, a lieutenant in the Royal Highland Regiment and a surveyor and engineer. Dugald was also the nephew of Patrick Campbell, the Scottish observer and writer. With neither civilians nor soldiery clamoring for land the survey, for a Loyalist settlement, was conducted with unaccustomed ease. Campbell followed Morris's instructions for the street layout to the letter. Around a large public square—part of which is now occupied by the old grave-yard—he laid out a grid of streets that overlapped the upriver end of the origi-nal townsite. Between the plat and the river, on the north side of the town, he set aside lands for government offices and the military. Lands on the remaining three sides of the plat were reserved for a college, the Church of England, and a free school or academy. In this way, reserved lands and river ringed the town.

Construction

Shelburne, Saint John, and St. Andrews, the most dynamic of the Loyalist towns, were such mushroom growths that observers from a world not yet accustomed to refugees were awed by them. Voicing the general sentiment, Colonel Robert Morse of the Royal Engineers thought them "astonishing" and ventured that they had been raised "in less time, perhaps, than was ever known in any country before." Joseph Aplin, who would become attorney general of Prince Edward Island, wrote of Saint John that "such an Instance of Sudden Exertion cannot be found in the Annals of any People on the Globe." During his ten day visit he saw such mighty scenes of industry and labour that he was "almost tempted to dis-credit [his] own eyes." At all the towns there were so many arrivals, or they came so late in the season, that there was little hope of housing them all securely before winter even if there had been enough town lots and enough materials for building. Loyalists who drew lots on arrival could begin work on their houses but the rest either had to stay on board the transports or put up makeshift shel-ters on commons, open land, or woods where they wouldn't interfere with the surveyors. Some, as the Reverend Jonathan Wiswall remarked of Shelburne, were living in huts "little if anything superior to the Cabins in Ireland." Shelter could sink no lower. To keep scurvy at bay, many dug clams and ate boiled dulse.

In Saint John, some of the provincials lived in "half-worn" tents donated by the British military while others "hutted" in the woods in crudely built log cab-ins. The most primitive shelters were made of poles covered with brush or bark or even scraps of sail canvas. Rooves, where no boards were available, were thatched with dry twigs, hay or overlapping, split tree trunks. Cracks, where there was no mud or mortar, were filled with moss. Even in St. Andrews, the most deliberate of the settlements, the Loyalists arrived so late in the season (late October) that most had to shift through the first winter. On his arrival in the winter of 1784 the Reverend Duncan McColl found civilians and soldiers living in bark huts and camping in deep snow in the surrounding woods.

For the first few years the Loyalist towns were an unsightly mixture of tents, shanties, wicker (wattle and daub) cottages, and log and frame houses. As settlers began to attend to their livings, to these were added shops, inns, workshops, taverns, coffee-houses and, in coastal towns, warehouses and wharves. It was the rash of houses, however, that caught the attention. As a sailor described Saint John: "numerous huts and houses scattered over the hills and rising grounds near the entrance of the river ... and great numbers of new wigwams, framed and log houses were continually beginning as the Settlers arrived."

Conditions were wretched in all the towns and perhaps at their worst in Birchtown, the black settlement in a rock-strewn woodland several miles northwest of Shelburne. Black Pioneers were among the first to arrive at Shelburne. Enlisted by the Chief Engineer Colonel Robert Morse, they helped with clearing the site and building public works: barracks, bridges, gaols, jetties etc. The engineer in charge of public works, Lieutenant Lawson, was authorized to use the Black labourers in any way he saw fit provided it was "in His Majesty's service only." In the 1780s, the notion of a freed Black was so novel that riders of this kind were necessary. Fearing reprisals or abuse, Governor Parr also felt bound to insist that Blacks be "considered as [part of] the human species." Never more than servants and labourers, they lived on the margins of Loyalist society.

In immediate charge of the Pioneers was Colonel Stephen Blucke, of mixed race, who assigned men to work in both Shelburne and Birchtown. In Shelburne itself the Blacks became scapegoats for Loyalist frustrations, a group of disbanded soldiers tearing down twenty of the Black Pioneers' houses on grounds that the freed Blacks were undercutting them in the labour market. Benjamin Marston reported that the Blacks seemed satisfied with their location in Birchtown but a White visitor found their circumstances "beyond description wretched. Situated on the coast in the middle of barren rocks, and partly surrounded by a thick, impenetrable wood ... I think I never saw such wretchedness and poverty so strongly perceptible in the garb and countenance of the human species as in these miserable outcasts."

Once settled on their lots, the inhabitants of the new towns could turn their minds to permanent housing. All settlements were entitled to draw on the king's provisions, which included building materials and tools as well as food and clothing, but supplies were usually inadequate and late. Lumber, too, could be bought from the Planters or from merchants in the New England ports. In general, however, it was so scarce that many houses were framed with logs, the available lumber being reserved for floors, partitions, windows and doors. Anticipating shortages in the new settlements, many Loyalists brought lumber with them, including door frames and windows, and a few even brought bricks. With the advantage of hindsight, several St. Andrews Loyalists went a step further, dismantling their Castine houses, numbering the parts for easy re-assembly, and rafting them across the Gulf of Maine to Passamaquoddy Bay and the mouth of the St. Croix.

As the surveys took effect the planned pattern of the towns began to emerge, the maze of tents and shanties giving way to an ordered arrangement of log and frame houses. Rates of building were remarkable. For all the complaints made about the laziness of the Shelburne Loyalists, Governor Parr, who had been one of their critics, was bound to admit that of all towns Shelburne was the "most expeditious that was ever built in so short a time." For a few years it was not only the largest town in Canada but the fourth largest in North America, exceeded only by New York, Boston, and Philadelphia. There was even talk of its becoming the capital of Nova Scotia and, in anticipation of this, Governor Parr set aside five hundred acres for himself outside the town. By December 1783, Parr could report that eight hundred houses were already fin-ished, six hundred more were "in great forwardness," and several hundred "lately begun upon." Besides houses there were, of course, wharves, inns, ware-houses and stores. From information gathered by Royal Engineers, Marston estimated that between May 23, 1783 and September, 1784, 1,127 buildings had been constructed. Of the dwellings, 80 were temporary winter shelters, 231 were framed houses, and the remainder log houses. Some of the latter were eventually shingled or clapboarded.

Saint John grew just as rapidly. By the middle of July 1783 about 400 houses had been built and by the end of September about 700. By early March of the following year there were about 1,500 framed houses and about 400 temporary ones made of hewn logs. In November 1784 James Putnam, writing to his broth-er John in Boston, was surprised to find "a large, flourishing town regularly laid out, well built, consisting of about two thousand houses, and many of them handsome and well-finished; and at the opposite side of the river, at Carleton, about 500 more houses on a pleasant situation."

Of the major Loyalist towns only Fredericton enjoyed the luxury of slow growth. A creation of government and the military rather than trade or com-merce, it was slow to become the metropolis envisaged by Governor Carleton. Until well after the turn of the century it remained a pleasant little country town in which the bishop used to pasture his cow on the cathedral grounds. In

1804, Lady Sir Martin Hunter was enchanted by it: "This is called a town, but is in fact a much prettier thing—a village, scattered on a delightful common of the richest sheep pasture I ever saw, and flocks grazing close up to our door. There are altogether about one hundred and twenty houses, some very pretty and comfortable-looking, and almost everyone has a garden."

In 1825, the historian Peter Fisher, who admired only the productive and useful, noted disapprovingly that the lands reserved for the support of the college and the church had not been much improved and were without tenants.

Fredericton waterfront c. 1825. In the left foreground is the old market house and in the right background, behind the trees, the officers quarters.

New Brunswick Museum

Until a few years before Fisher's visit, church and college lands had been held under perpetual leases, the leaseholders making annual rent payments. But in 1817 the discovery of an English law forbidding colleges from making conveyances of any sort rendered perpetual leases invalid. Development of college lands came to a halt, as did the outward growth of the town. In 1852 a Fredericton editor complained bitterly that large endowments for the church, the college and the military combined with large grants to a few individuals had left the youthful town "as naked as a rock on a common." But in truth, the freezing of the church and college lands was no great stricture. By 1832

Fredericton might have lost its village-like look but to an English visitor the settlement was still no more than "two principal streets running parallel with the river, and containing about twelve hundred inhabitants." Although the visitor underestimated the population by more than a thousand, the figure stood at only 4,000 in 1840. Far from restricting growth, confinement within the town plat for so small a population ensured a more compact and orderly settlement than might otherwise have developed.

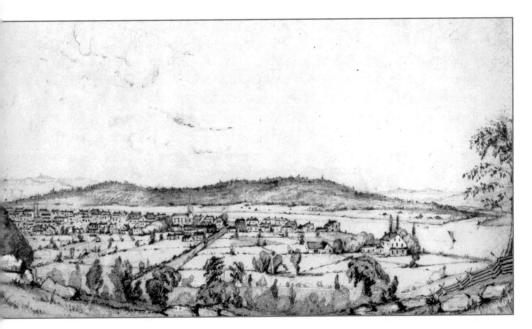

Fredericton from College Hill, 1837 (William Robert Herries).

House Design

A series of wash drawings of Shelburne by Captain William Booth show a variety of houses and commercial buildings. The buildings are rectangular, between one and two-and-a-half storeys high, with high peaked gable ends or—if a little extra height was needed—gambrel roofs. Exteriors are covered with shingles or clapboards. Gables are eaveless and door and window casings are made of plain finishing boards. There is little evidence of paint. Yet the buildings, though plain, are far from graceless. Windows are small paned, double hung, and in some cases shuttered; doors are four- or six-panelled Christian doors and several are crowned with fanlights for lighting the hallways within. Both doors and windows are well proportioned and so arranged that facades are pleasingly symmetrical. Interior walls were panelled with pine or oak boards or roughly plastered and then coated with a smooth wash of lime. It is known, too, that some wallpaper was available.

From the outset it was apparent that neither Shelburne nor the other Loyalist towns would remain makeshift pioneer settlements for long. Unlike later migrants to North America, the Loyalists had come to replace a world they had lost, not experiment with a new one. They were also people of a common culture and, as such, subject to unspoken restraints that prevented great deviations from what was considered normal or acceptable. To these unofficial restraints they, as devotees of law and order, added official ones designed to enhance the safety and the appearance of their settlements. To reduce damage by fire, and to discourage the building of mean houses and shanties, lot sizes were generous (usually 80 feet by 160 feet) and streets wide (60 feet for side streets and 80 feet for main). A notice in a September 1784 issue of the *Saint John Gazette*, inserted

Captain William Booth's sketch of Shelburne, 1789. On the far shore is the officers' barracks. National Archives of Canada.

National Archives of Canada

by the director of the town of Carleton, warned that the owners of lots who ignored the conditions of clearing, fencing and building would be liable to forfeit. In St. Andrews buildings of set dimensions and solid structure had to be built within a year otherwise the lots had to be given up. In the interests of neat, orderly streetscapes, Fredericton's regulations decreed that houses were to be built on the front edge of the lot, and in the centre. Any space in front of an eighteenth century house would have been a muddy quagmire where horses were tied and carriages parked, not a neat lawn.

In short, there were to be no permanent shanties and, unlike the towns of the western frontier, no ramshackle buildings hiding behind false fronts. In

A vernacular style salt-box house in St. Andrews, New Brunswick. Local tradition has it that at least the front part of the house was brought prefabricated from Castine, Maine, by Joseph Crookshank, a ship's carpenter.

Private collection

Fredericton and St. Andrews all houses were to be at least twenty feet wide by sixteen deep. In Fredericton, too, privies were to be at the backs of the houses, no lanes were to cross the building lots, and, for fear of fire, there were to be no thatched roofs. Fire prevention was a preoccupation in all the towns. At Shelburne one of the first acts of the magistrates was to appoint fire wards, name the directors of chimney sweeps, and set fees for sweeping. Chimneys were to be swept regularly once a month.

House design was a matter for the owner but there were few departures from accepted norms. For the ordinary folk in the towns, the standard house was a Cape Cod cottage or a variation thereof. The initial house for many would have been a small, single storey rectangular building with a gable roof and a loft—the folk or vernacular house of the eastern seaboard and much of England. A few Connecticut salt box houses were built in New Brunswick but an organic form that probably grew out of the primitive lean-to had no great appeal for the Loyalists. A well-constructed "Cape" on the other hand was a formal building with a respectable pedigree; its immediate relations were the cottages of seventeenth-century East Anglia. A standard Cape was frame-built, roughly square in shape, with a central chimney and stairway and a second storey nestled beneath a steeply pitched gabled roof. Parlours, bedrooms, and a large kitchen were arranged neatly on each side of the chimney and stairway. Exteriors simply heralded the order within. Doorways were central in the facade and windows were well proportioned and evenly spaced. Trim, if any, was restrained and economical; doorways were unadorned except for fanlights,

and eaves and gable ends were spare and plain. Shingles, rather than clapboards, were the usual covering for both walls and roof. Low walls and tight eaves made for ease and efficiency of heating while the massive chimney and large roof gave the house a snug, sheltering look. These were critical attributes in a climate the Loyalists found inhospitable.

For their permanent houses (often built several years after the initial settlement), the wealthier Loyalists usually opted for a more deliberate "British" style: two-storey Georgian townhouses often designed from English pattern books. The hallmarks of the style were compact, rectangular shapes, and balanced facades: usually a central doorway, often with sidelights as well as a fan-

Left and above photos: The Putnam House, Fredericton. Above: a formal Georgian house with the standard five bays, a central hallway and portico, and four chimneys arranged symmetrically on the outside corners. The house was built c.1807 (George Neilson Smith, 1842).

(left) New Brunswick Museum, (above) The Beaverbrook Art Gallery, Fredericton, N.B.

light, and well-proportioned windows arranged symmetrically on each side of the door. On the second floor, five bays (windows) were standard. In the more elegant houses windows were shuttered, fanlights arched, doorways moulded and often porticoed, and gables and eaves generous. Conspicuously absent, however, were the grand, architecturally framed doorways then popular in the United States and the projections and additions often found in English houses. Anxious to avoid the taint of Republican ideology, Maritime Loyalists also resisted the grand, Roman-inspired neoclassical building style then in vogue in the seaboard states. But the greatest restraining factor of all, perhaps, was not politics but poverty. By American standards the Maritime Loyalists were poor and, and as any journey into the seaboard states will demonstrate, they built fewer large houses and even their standard houses were smaller and more austere.

As in the United States, exteriors of the houses were generally of claboard and only occasionally of the more impressive brick, which was, of course, more expensive. Interiors were just as regular as these exteriors, and each floor had a pair of rooms (of roughly equal size) on each side of the usually spacious central hallway and staircase. Banished, though, were the central chimney and the dominant kitchen of the Cape Cod houses.

The Cossit House in Sydney built ca. 1787 by Rev. Ranna Cossit, a Loyalist and the first Anglican minister in Sydney. The house is now a part of the Nova Scotia Museum Complex.

Communications Nova Scotia

In 1787, instructions for an early and relatively plain townhouse were left by George Sproule, New Brunswick's surveyor-general, to Jared Betts, a Fredericton builder and developer. Sproule agreed to rent the house only if it was designed and finished in a manner that fitted his rank and predilections. The main or ground floor was to consist of three rooms and a hall, "seven feet wide," through the house. At least two rooms were to open from the hall: a dining room on the right, connected to a kitchen, and on the left a drawing room connected to a bedroom. Each of the ground floor rooms was to have a chimney and be "well finished with lath and plaister and papered over the whole." The first floor was to be "fitted up into two bed chambers with a chimney to each." These, too, were to be properly lathed, plastered and papered and each was to have sashed windows and paneled doors with knob-locks. A passage lighted with a dormer window was to run between the bedrooms. It would connect, via a short flight of steps, to two garret rooms for servants at the back of house.

Although English in essentials, Loyalist houses, unlike English townhouses, were freestanding; neither in the Maritimes nor New England were there resi-

Built as a garrison church in 1785, St. Georges Church in Sydney also served the Anglican Loyalist community.

Beaton Institute, University College of Cape Breton

dential terraces or squares. To reduce the danger from fire, the houses were built equidistant from the sides of the lot and for greater regularity they were, like English townhouses, built on or, as a Fredericton town ordinance ruled, "even in line with the street." In St. Andrews the houses had to be "exactly six feet from the Street." A few of the older houses showed their gable ends to the street, with the main entrance opening onto a lawn or an enclosed garden, but houses of the higher class invariably looked outward. With no long setbacks or sanitary lawns between the house and the street—a general requirement of nineteenth century planning in North America—the Loyalist towns have an old world look. But because the houses usually stand alone, rather than in continuous terraces or rows, there was rarely any feeling of an enclosed urban space of the traditional European type. Streets were also wide, 60-80 feet in most towns, and where gardens were not threatened by grazing animals properties were often unfenced, reinforcing the feeling of an open rather than an enclosed urbanism.

Classically proportioned houses laid out authoritatively along straight generous streets satisfied the need for order and good taste, both of which were vitally important to the Loyalists. Although town plans and house styles had been funneled through New England and the middle colonies they still carried old world associations. The symmetry and solidity of the houses, combined with the regularity of the streets, also suggested a measure of human control in what was, in effect, raw wilderness. In an environment that at every turn reminded them of their frailty and limitations, a regularly planned town or even a well-proportioned house was reassuring. The psychological comfort they gave may explain why, in colonial samplers and folk paintings, a solid, Georgian house standing four square to the elements was such a popular motif.

Interiors and Social Life

The elegance of the larger townhouses was not just a matter of exteriors; interiors were also carefully designed and finished. Rooms were well-proportioned and in houses they were arranged symmetrically on each side of a central hallway and staircase. Doors, window cases, mantles and stair rails were invariably delicate and finely made. The more prosperous Loyalists brought their furnishings with them so that the larger houses might have had fine mahogany chairs, tables and desks, silver and glassware, imported English wallpapers, books, and in a few cases, extensive libraries. A gloss of civility and refinement not only put the wilderness in its place but served to foil the republican distrust of finery and polite society. If unchecked these, so some republicans believed, would threaten moral character. Thus future President John Adams's remarkable diatribe: "It would produce so much taste and politeness, so much elegance in dress, furniture, equipage, so much music and dancing, so much fencing and skating, so much cards and backgammon; so much horse racing and cockfighting, so many balls and assemblies, so many plays and concerts that the very imagination of them makes me feel vain, light, frivolous, and insignificant." Tory finery had also been the focus of popular republican anger. Few Bostonians would ever forget the systematic destruction of Governor Hutchinson's mansion house by a mob protesting the Stamp Act. In a rage that lasted till dawn, clothing, plate, hangings, manuscripts, and even money were destroyed; doors were axed, wainscots and wall hangings ripped off, furniture smashed, and formal gardens torn up.

The garden and slave ell of the Jonathan O'Dell House, Fredericton. There were two sleeping lofts, one for each sex, with seperate staircases.

George Thomas Taylor, Public Archives of New Brunswick

The need for refinement or "respectability" was also reflected in manners and social life. But some visitors found it exaggerated and gauche. The American Charles Turner noted that Gabriel Ludlow, the Mayor of Saint John, greeted a visiting party "with as much politeness as we could expect from a provincial aping the hauteur of the British." Colonel Gubbins also thought it a case of country cousins mimicing metropolitan ways and manners. But for a frontier society even to have aspired to social graces was in itself remarkable. Remarkable, too, was the determination not to let uprooting deprive them of the pleasures of a social life. In Halifax, Penelope Winslow described the life of her friends as a round of feasting, card playing, and dancing: "pursuing pleasure with ardour."

The pursuit of pleasure, dancing in particular, earned Shelburne Loyalists the title of "the Dancing Beggars." In Shelburne no occasion for a celebratory feast or ball seems to have been missed: royal birthdays, the anniversaries of military victories, and the visitations of even minor dignitaries were occasions, or pretexts, for dances and balls. The town's first official dance, a bonfire-lit

A postcard of the Old Firth House, Shelburne, built in 1785. From this house Governor Parr, in 1784, re-named Port Roseway to honour Lord Shelburne.

Public Archives of Nova Scotia

affair held amongst the stumps and shanties a month after the landing, celebrated the King's birthday. A ball at McGragh's tavern in January 1784 to honour the Queen's birthday found 50 gentlemen and ladies dancing, drinking and playing cards in a house situated where six months previously there had been an almost impenetrable swamp. At a ball convened the following July, to entertain Governor Parr when he named the town for his patron Lord Shelburne, "the ladies danced till nearly five." So popular was dancing that one private school in Shelburne offered, in addition to the three R's and classics, twice-weekly dancing lessons for "the young Ladies and Gentlemen." The licence, however, did not extend to Black Loyalists; in May, 1785, the authorities distributed handbills forbidding "Negro Dances and Negro Frolicks in the town of Shelburne." Yet the frolics continued, and a year later constables were ordered to arrest Blacks found dancing and gambling at night.

The penchant for such behaviour in Shelburne was so exceptional, not to say scandalous that a former district judge turned Halifax merchant could make it the subject of a sketch, "Shelburnian Manners." He felt no admiration for the inhabitants of Shelburne, who "from the highest to the lowest have a pitiable passion for finery, revelling & dancing & every species of instant gratification." Benjamin Marston, who found himself surveying lots—probably unassisted— while the populace danced, was also critical. He complained of no work being done on the king's birthday and for several days afterward. Governor Parr voiced a similar grievance in 1784: "The inhabitants vie with each other in making fine appearances, which in the present state of things they cannot long support." While their betters danced, rank-and-file Loyalists were packed several families to a house, crowded into transport ships, and confined to tents, shacks, warehouses, and church basements. In Halifax there were even bread lines.

Although Saint John was merely a pair of small towns on the margins of the wilderness, its social leaders were at pains to emphasize that they yielded nothing to Halifax gentry in the sophistication of their entertainments and the elegance of their dress. One refugee enthused about a "most agreeable ball" held at the remarkably early date of August 15, 1783. Two winters later the entertainments were in full swing. In a letter to John Wentworth, Edward Winslow noted that "till this winter [1785–86] I had no idea of the jollity and sociability which a good neighborhood may enjoy in the coldest of weather." It was a view endorsed by Mather Byles, who passed that same winter at Edward Winslow's house, Felicity Hall: "I never," he wrote to his sisters at Halifax, "expect to see a more agreeable collection of people about me than I have at present."

If a town was garrisoned with regular British army units as, for varying periods, were Fredericton, Saint John, Shelburne, and St. Andrews, then social life was even more colourful. Fredericton, the most military of the Loyalist towns, was home to British army units for 84 years. For the first 40 of these soldiers and their dependents must sometimes have outnumbered civilian residents. Peacetime postings were not demanding and, for the officers at least, they left ample time for recreation and entertainment. James Glenie, the *bête noir* of New Brunswick's social and political establishment, considered Fredericton's military role to be vastly overrated: an entire regiment, as he put it acerbically, having nothing to do but "[maintain] guard on the Governor's farm." As a rule, officers entered fully into the social life of the community, many finding wives in the process. Private soldiers, on the other hand, tended to be social outcasts, relegated to the back and upper pews of the Anglican churches and to the fringes of society. The "miasma of immorality," as one observer put it, emanating from a thousand idle men at the Fredericton barracks, gave local matrons pause. But instead of the matrons having to lock up their daughters, the military locked up the men. Surrounding the barracks was a 14-foot-high pallisade made of posts, as Patrick Campbell described them in 1792, "so strait and close that a cat cannot get through; and so firmly set as to secure everything within, like a rampart."

Provincial militias, too, which became increasingly prominent as more and more British troops were assigned to the Napoleonic War, were heavily social. Although every man between 16 and 60 was expected to turn up with a good musket, bayonet, and belt cartridge at the first beat of the drums of war, in practice militias were more social and ceremonial than functional. Militia officers, who were usually veterans of the Revolutionary war, were the leading fig-

Officers quarters, Fredericton, after a flood. Taylor's interest in photography stemmed from articles in English periodicals loaned to him by officers of the garrison (George Thomas Taylor).

Public Archives of New Brunswick

ures in their communities and their houses often the scene of entertainments. Chestnut Hall in St. Andrews, the house of militia colonel Harris Hatch, was renowned for lavish entertainments crowned by sumptuous meals prepared by Violet, Colonel Hatch's Black cook.

Decline of the Towns

Merrymaking in towns that were little more than construction sites might be interpreted as an act of bold defiance, a gallant determination to preserve a certain gaiety in the face of privation and, in the case of some of the settlements, impending disaster. The withdrawal of the King's Allowance in 1787 and the removal of the residence requirement from half-pay pensions sent a tremor through many of the Loyalist settlements. No longer bound to British North America by free government provisions or, in the case of half-pay officers, by the need to live within the Empire, many chose to leave. Some made for England, the Bahamas, and the West Indies, but most simply went home. Tempers had cooled and returning Loyalists were tolerated and even welcomed. In Nova Scotia, where levels of dissatisfaction were particularly high, both rural areas and towns lost population, and land and property values declined. Digby was spoken of as "yearly decreasing and in danger of total Dissolution" while Manchester (later Guysborough), which in 1783 had 200 dwellings, however makeshift, by 1815 was reduced to five houses and three barns. Immigrant Scots, English and Irish would eventually make up the deficits but so alarming was the exodus that in 1789 the Nova Scotia Assembly passed an act preventing people from leaving the colony without a pass.

The most spectacular losses were suffered by Shelburne, the most volatile—and the most vulnerable—of the Loyalist towns. Beguiled by its magnificent

Militia drilling outside Fredericton, 1865.

Public Archives of New Brunswick

harbour, and its accessibilty from Britain and the West Indies, the Loyalist agents had overlooked all the deficiencies of the site. There was no land for farming, no substantial timber resources nearby, and no large navigable river to tap the timber resources of the interior. Once the local lumber had been cut, Shelburne found itself without a hinterland to provide either products for export or markets for imports. Nor, without roads or a navigable river, was there any possibility of acquiring one. A notice in the *Royal American Gazette*

Militia drilling outside the old Market Hall, St. Andrews.

Public Archives of New Brunswick

in the 1780s was a measure of the town's desperation: "It is of the utmost consequence to the prosperity of this settlement, that immediate and extensive communications should be opened as speedily as possible to the other cultivated parts of the province, and to Annapolis in particular."

Roads to Annapolis or elsewhere never materialized and the exodus began. First to leave were the surrounding farmers who, after the long wait to get their grants, were confronted with land that was uncultivable and farms that were sometimes, as in the case of those laid out along a hypothetical road across the peninsula to Annapolis, located capriciously. Surfaces tended to be either swampy and wet, or dry and stone-filled. Captain William Booth's assessment of the country around Shelburne was a "valley with much stones and a little swampy." It was also littered with fallen trees and moss. Once tons of rock had been lifted, potatoes, vegetables, and the hardy cereals could be grown and—

provided there were pastures and meadowlands—cattle raised, but there was no possibility of soil so "unfriendly," as a distraught Gideon White described it, ever rewarding farmers or supporting a large town. For Captain Booth the farmers were victims of "expectations far too exalted" and by 1789, as he noted, most of them were "off or at least very few remaining."

Fishing, too, was a disappointment. Although easy at first—"fish was never more plenty not easier come at, than from this place"—the Shelburne Loyalists quickly discovered that there was more to successful codfishing than baiting hooks in cod-infested waters. A few men in a boat might catch hundreds of cod in a day but to be marketed the cod had to be be dried, salted and packed, skills the Shelburne men lacked. Hopes rose in 1784 with the arrival of a few experienced New England fishermen but the introduction failed to produce either the quantity or the quality of fish required. The boats were small and badly fitted, obliging the fishermen to hug the shores where fish were small, but even with the best gear the ways of fish and the sea could not be learned overnight. Good fishing at Shelburne called for a ten-mile tack to the harbour's mouth and a still farther sail to the fishing grounds. Shelburne Harbour, too, was so far from open water that moored vessels were subject to damage by grinding ice.

Given the handicaps, Shelburne fishermen were no match for their cousins in the New England ports whose superior experience, they conceded, "precludes us from becoming their rivals." Nor, too, could they compete with Newfoundlanders who by 1787 were flooding the West Indian market with dried and salted cod. Defeated, most Shelburne fishermen put up their lines and nets and those merchants who continued to trade in fish loaded their vessels in Newfoundland. Shelburne would eventually (in the 1840s) profit from fishing, but in 1805 the town had only one registered fishing boat.

Whaling also failed. Requiring only "people dextrous in killing the whale" and not on "proper dressing and curing," it promised to be a less complicated trade than the cod fishery. Involving distant seas and overseas markets, it was also more alluring to mercantile temperaments. The target was the Brazilian fishery, and the market—for spermacetti and oil—was London. Whales were caught and oil delivered in vessels built and financed by Shelburne merchants but as the product of foreign vessels the oil was subject to high rates of duty. Great Britain refused to grant a colonial exemption and by 1790 the Shelburne Whale Fishing Company, unable to compete with British whalers, had folded. At the same time the owners of private whaling vessels also left Shelburne.

The failure of farming and the cod and whale fisheries were damaging blows, but not mortal ones. Like St. Andrews and Saint John, Shelburne had hitched its wagon to an imperial star—to the empire of the Atlantic and British mercantilist policies. While Americans looked west to a new, continental world beyond the Appalachians, Loyalists looked east to Britain and the Atlantic and to the protection of Britain's Navigation laws. The Loyalists' grand plan for the Maritimes was to take over from the Americans the carrying trade with the West Indies. Edward Winslow had boasted to the Board of Trade that Maritime waters and woods could supply the West Indies with all the fish and lumber they could possibly need. Not only this, but each of the Loyalist ports had merchants experienced in overseas trade and with well-established contacts with trading houses in England, the West Indies, and Europe. Shelburne vessels scoured the ports of Nova Scotia, New England, and Newfoundland in search of outward bound cargoes: dried and pickled fish, barrel staves, shingles, boards, square timbers, ship's knees, and furs that could be exchanged for West Indian sugar, tobacco, rum, and molasses. From England came finished goods and manufactures: hogsheads of porter, gloves, hair ribbons, hardware, pewter, brass, copper, and umbrellas.

From the outset, trade at Shelburne was conducted almost entirely by barter. There was a great shortage of cash and Shelburne merchants were well aware that there was little possibility of generating any locally; the town itself they regarded as a "very uncertain and trifling market by no means calculated to carry on any scrape of Business without hazard." Everything depended on their monopoly of the Atlantic carrying trade and, given England's conciliatory attitude toward Americans and the pressure from West Indian Planters for the unrestrained entry of American goods, there was no guarantee of its continuation. So nervous was the town, and so hungry its newspapers for English views on the West Indian and American trade, that the *Halifax Gazette* depended on the Shelburne papers for its foreign news. Anxieties abated in 1785 when American vessels were rigidly excluded from the West Indies but rose again once Americans found ways of evading or modifying the Navigation Laws. In 1788 American vessels were allowed to carry fish to the islands, a concession that "during stress or emergency" extended to all goods. After 1788 there was a sharp increase in the incidence of Caribbean storms.

For Shelburne merchants and shippers there were also enemies within. Yielding to complaints that local products were too costly, the Governor and Council opened Nova Scotian ports to American vessels. Protests from Shelburne and elsewhere brought about a repeal but in retaliation Massachusetts imposed a duty of ten shillings per ton on all British vessels loading at any port in the state. Reeling from duties on exports and imports as well as duties in foreign ports, Shelburne merchants, who had spent their capital building vessels, stores, warehouses, wharves, and houses, appealed for a ten-year exemption from all taxes and duties until the town was established. Failing this, they asked that any taxes collected at least remain within Shelburne "for the distinct use and benefit of the town." Halifax responded by setting up a customs house in Shelburne, the only one outside the capital, but it was a case of too little too late. As a trading settlement Shelburne was doomed.

To make matters even worse, Shelburne also lost its garrison and its Black workers. In spite of "all the advantages attending the harbour," Colonel Robert Morse of the Royal Engineers did not think it an "eligible one from a military point of view." As an army base it was too isolated to be useful and as a navy base it was too difficult to defend, the entrance at the mouth of the harbour being too wide to be secured by batteries. The departing soldiers were soon followed by Black workers who had been bullied, denied land, and even the right to dance. Some drifted to Halifax and other towns but most, about 800, joined the exodus to Sierra Leone.

Had the Shelburne Loyalists proceeded cautiously, the damage inflicted by the failure of farming, fishing, and long-distance trade, might have been reduced, but hardly averted. As their detractors were quick to point out, they had paid the penalty for spending unwisely, for pouring money into elaborate houses, hotels, coffee houses and stores before they had devised a means or an economy to support them. "The inhabitants," wrote Oliver Wiswell, "vie with each other in making fine appearances, which in the present state of things they cannot long support." William Chew of Maugerville made the same point more pithily: "Your town exceeds ours I believe in size, but what's a fine house without something to put in it." For the modern historian Ian MacKinnon, Shelburne's folly was a case of investing capital in lifestyle, not livelihood. Once investment capital salvaged from the war had been exhausted then the cracks in the town's armour became gaping holes. "All commerce is at a stand," wrote a contributor to the *London Chronicle* as early as 1784 "and the very large sums of money they brought from New York are nearly exhausted, without having fixed upon any staple commodity....When the King's bounty to the Loyalists shall cease, it is a mystery, to what hand they can turn themselves for the means of subsistence."

Few towns have collapsed so quickly and so completely as Shelburne. Within months of its founding, all the measures of economic well-being pointed to decline. Population plummeted from a high of perhaps 9,000 in 1784 to 3,000 in 1788 and about 400 in 1820. Anticipating defections, in 1784 Governor Patterson of Prince Edward Island posted a proclamation on the streets of Shelburne offering land from his personal holdings on the same terms as Nova Scotia and Quebec. By midsummer several hundred refugees and disbanded troops were ready to sail for the Island. Others moved to New Brunswick, England, and the West Indies but most simply went back to the States. Naval Office reports of ships entering and leaving Shelburne tell a similar story. In 1787, from July 1 to December 31, sixty-five ships entered Shelburne and sixty-nine were cleared; in 1789, from January 1 to June 30, thirty entered and thirty-two were cleared; and from Oct. 1, 1789, to March 31, 1790, six entered and seven were cleared. At the Shelburne customs house duties collected fell from 1,380 pounds in 1788 to 431 pounds in 1789.

As its life-blood seeped away, the body of the town atrophied and slowly crumbled. By 1789 two-thirds of the buildings were unoccupied. So rapid was the exodus that it resembled a town struck by plague rather than ill-considered

The Ross-Thomson house and warehouse, Shelburne, before restoration. The attached buildings were built by the brothers George and Robert Ross in 1785 and sold to fellow merchant Robert Thomson in 1815. The dwelling is on the right. The brothers, who shared a common dining room, had separate apartments on the ground and upper floors. The slaves slept in the attic.

Public Archives of Nova Scotia

investment. Writing of Shelburne in 1826, Thomas Haliburton noted that "the houses were still standing, though untenanted. It was difficult to imagine that the place was deserted. The idea of repose more readily suggested itself than decay." But decay inevitably followed. Buildings with taxes unpaid were advertised for sale and if not sold and deemed a fire hazard they were demolished. Thirty or forty years later strangers marvelled at the grass-grown streets, broken cellar holes, and wharves falling into the water—all tragic proof as Marion Robertson, Shelburne's historian reminds us, that towns are not built without hinterlands and without planning and resolution.

Like Shelburne, St. Andrews had also cast its lot with the Empire of the Atlantic. Located at the tip of a long, narrow peninsula at the mouth of the St. Croix River, it depended entirely on its commercial sea links with the West Indies, Britain, and the United States. If these were broken the town, which had no hinterland, would be be left without support. For tapping the timber resources of the St. Croix, the neighbouring town of St. Stephen, at the head of

The Ross-Thomson warehouse and store is the only commercial survival from the initial phase of building. Goods were hoisted onto the second floor which, to provide extra storage space, has a gambrel roof. The dwelling is hip-roofed.

Public Archives of Nova Scotia

navigation, was far better placed. Patrick Campbell, that astute Scottish observer, saw the dangers of protectionism and an isolated location when he visited in 1794. He allowed that St. Andrews was prettily situated, with a good harbour, and that it had "a smart trade in ship building, lumber, and fish," but feared that the prosperity would last only as long as Americans were kept out of British and colonial markets. Once they were allowed in, he predicted that St. Andrews would become "a desert" and that its people would settle elsewhere.

A view of the Shelburne waterfront, 1899.

Supported by British provisions and with an active trade in lumber and fish to the West Indies, the town then was in no immediate danger. Separated from the United States only by a bay and a tangle of islands, it also had a flourishing carrying trade, passing goods "along the lines" between British and American shippers, who were forbidden to trade directly with each other when their countries were at odds or at war. The first blow fell in 1830, when Britain announced its intention of repealing the Navigation Laws and opening West Indian markets to American shipping. Even the prospect of unlimited quantities of cheaper American goods was enough to leave laden Maritime vessels stranded in tropical harbours. The value of St. Andrews' exports to the West Indies fell from £104,000 in 1829 (roughly two thirds of its annual exports) to £36,000 in 1834. At the same time that Yankee traders were "crowding in" on West Indian markets, lumber exports to Britain were falling off. The British market remained protected until 1842, but, by this time, lumbering on the St. Croix had moved well upstream. There were still marketable trees around St. Andrews, but most were in tracts held by the Royal Navy.

The loss of the British and the West Indian market was a disastrous blow. From being an important link in the commerce of the Atlantic, St. Andrews suddenly found itself in the remote corner of a continent that had turned its back on Europe and the West Indies. With its shipping and lumber trade gone, and with no hinterland to draw on, the town was in dire straits. It managed to stay neat and trim but as early as 1836 its trade, as the historian Peter Fisher noted, "appear[ed] to be dwindling away without any satisfactory prospect of revival." To stop the rot a group of businessmen struck on the vaulting idea of making St. Andrews the winter port of Canada by building a railway to Quebec. Funds were raised and a route surveyed but work on the project halted when the Americans discovered that the builders intended running it through territory then in dispute between Maine and New Brunswick. The Webster/Ashburton Treaty of 1842 settled the dispute, but not before Saint John and Halifax had both decided that they, too, would make excellent Atlantic termini. Construction of the St. Andrews/Quebec line began in 1847 but the line, as projected, was never completed.

For St. Andrews, the railway to the interior, which promised to marry the new continental economy to the old Atlantic one, was its last fling at a vital, workaday existence. In 1860, a visitor returning after a twelve year interval found the town to be "dull, dilapidated, and in need of paint." Idle men, looking like "shipwrecked sailors on a deserted isle," sauntered dejectedly about the streets and wharves, and a shore that once was alive with sail became a catchpit for unwanted schooners and barges. As the town's economy collapsed people drifted away. By 1880 the population was fewer than two thousand, perhaps a half of the figure at the beginning of the century. The town would survive but, like Shelburne, its vitality had gone.

Of the major Loyalist towns only Fredericton and Saint John enjoyed growth. Fredericton had a slow start but as a garrison town, the seat of government, and service and market centre for the richest section of the valley, its future was secure. Saint John, too, would clearly survive. At the mouth of a great river system and as the funnel for the huge lumber resources of the valley, it was bound to be an important mercantile city. As such it was subject to the uncertainties of international and long-distance trade. Like St. Andrews it suffered from the loss to the Americans of the West Indies market, from the repeal of the Navigation Laws, the dropping of the colonial preference in the lumber trade, and the decline of wooden shipbuilding. It also suffered a succession of devastating

Saint John, looking west across the harbour, 1860s-70s.

William R. Notman. National Archives of Canada.

Top right: King Street, Saint John's main commercial street, 1867-73. At the foot of the street is Market Slip, the town wharf and site of the Loyalist landing in 1783.

National Archives of Canada

Left: The "Great Conflagration" of 1837 was the first of a series of fires, culminating in the great fire of 1877, that destroyed most of Loyalist Saint John. The painting, by William Henry Wentworth, 1838, is based on an eyewitness sketch by Thomas H. Wentworth.

The Beaverbrook Art Gallery, Fredericton, N.B.

fires and, after Confederation, a national economic policy that, in Maritime eyes, left her a Cinderella at the mercy of her more powerful continental sisters. A less resilient city might have wasted away, but in cities, as in real estate, location is everything. The valley and the New Brunswick shore of the Bay of Fundy needed a fulcrum—an organizing, marketing, and supply centre—and there was no better place for it than the two rocky headlands at the mouth of the Saint John River.

Chapter Three

Public
and Official
Buildings

I n designing their public and official buildings, people whose feet were in the new world, but whose heads were in the old, looked naturally to Britain. Eighteenth century British architecture, by returning to rules of proportion, harmony, and scale laid down in classical Greece and Rome had, in the eyes of classicists such as Horace Walpole, "resumed all her rights." For official buildings required to express public authority and serve, in colonial territories, as symbols of order and control, there could not have been a more suitable style. It was an architecture tailor-made for empire builders and its use became so habitual that colonial officials could hardly conceive of employing any other. When Governor Thomas Carleton built his mansion house just outside Fredericton he turned automatically to English classicism. The house (built in 1787) was destroyed by fire in 1815 but a surviving painting and a description by General Sir Martin Hunter point to a grand house with a classical facade.

Even grander was Sir John Wentworth's new Government House in Halifax. On succeeding Sir John Parr as Governor of Nova Scotia, in 1792, Wentworth, the first Loyalist governor, began to campaign for a new residence. The existing one, said to have been built hurriedly from green lumber and, like other buildings in Halifax, painted to look like freestone was, Wentworth complained, so damp and cold that it affected both his wife's health and his own. The country members of the provincial assembly, who wanted roads, not public buildings in Halifax, demurred, but Wentworth's persistence finally wore them down. In

1798 they agreed to build a new governor's residence, of stone not wood, on a plot of land in the south suburbs of the city. Wentworth, who wanted an estate with formal gardens, stables and a coach house, not just a large house, was delighted with the arrangement. Apart from the governor's residence, there were then no public buildings in Halifax, the Assembly and the courts meeting in rented rooms.

The architect and master builder for the new house, Isaac Hildreth, was a Yorkshireman who came to Halifax via Virginia and—as a Loyalist—Shelburne. At Shelburne he designed and built Christ Church, the first Anglican church. For ideas for the new Government House Hildreth and Wentworth looked to England, modifying a design from George Richardson's book, *A Series of Designs for County Seats*. For 18 years Richardson had worked as a draughtsman and designer for Robert Adam, the father of English classicism. The fruit of the Hildreth-Wentworth collaboration was a house of classic proportions: a centre block three storeys high, with a central doorway and five bays (five windows), flanked by two wings. The cornerstone was laid on September 11, 1800, to the strains of "God Save the King" and "Rule Britannia" played by an attendant band. Then followed an earnest and, if reported correctly, convoluted Loyalist prayer: that God grant that "this Monument of the increasing Prosperity of the infant Colony, may hand down to the latest Posterity, the loyalty and attachment of its Inhabitants to the best of Sovereigns, and their affection and regard for those who were, at that Period, placed in authority under him."

With its governor properly housed, Nova Scotia could now give its attention to its homeless legislature. The architect for Province House (1811-1819) was John Merrick, a master painter who had been

Top right: Portraits of John Wentworth, Lt.-Governor of Nova Scotia 1792 to 1808 and his wife Francis.

John Singleton Copley: (left) Government House, Halifax; (right) New York Public Library

Government House, Halifax, 1819.

John Elliott Woolford, National Archives of Canada

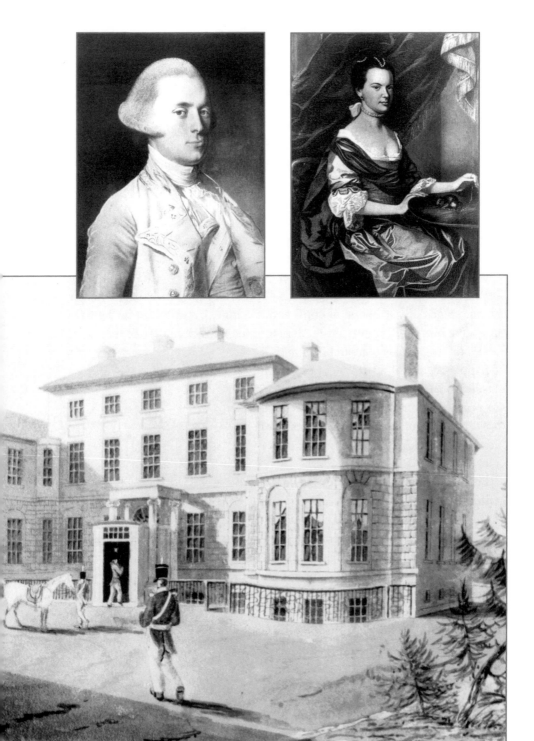

responsible for the interior decoration of the Governor's residence. When Charles Dickens visited Halifax in 1842 he called Merrick's building, thought to have been based on a plan procured in England, "a gem of Georgian architecture." Merrick's design, as Harold Kalman has pointed out, became a sort of British standard, a model for legislative buildings in other Maritime provinces, and for town halls throughout British North America. Unlike classical revival public buildings in American cities, consciously modelled after Greek temples, Province House was a British mutation that would have fitted comfortably into Bath or Edinburgh's New Town.

The British classical style was also the chosen form for barracks, courthouses, and other public buildings. In both Fredericton and Shelburne, the officers' quarters were models of Georgian elegance. A sketch of the Shelburne barracks shows classically proportioned buildings set incongruously—like the town itself—in a wilderness of stumps and rocks. In a letter to Lord Sydney, General Campbell complained that "the expense of those barracks has been enormous, owing, principally to the situation—about a mile, by water, from the town—they have been built upon." In Fredericton, the barrack master of the garrison,

J.E. Woolford, was also an architect and, it so happened, a prolific exponent of British classicism. In short order, he designed Government House (1828), King's College (now the Arts Building of the University of New Brunswick, 1829), and York County Gaol (1830).

Like governors' houses and legislative buildings, courthouses were also potent symbols of British authority. City courthouses, such as John Cunningham's courthouse in Saint John, were built of cut stone (ashlar) but in the smaller shire or county towns the gravitas that law and government require had to be achieved in wood and at a fraction of the cost. The most striking of the smaller courthouses is the one at St. Andrews, not built until the accession of

A perspective view of Province House,
Halifax, from the northeast. (J.E. Woolford)

An architectural elevation of Province House, Halifax (John Elliott Woolford).

National Archives of Canada.

Victoria, but which carefully preserves classical forms. In his determination to make it one of the finest courthouses in the province and, as he put it, a true symbol of British culture, the builder Thomas Berry exceeded his budget by several hundred pounds, a large sum at the time. To emphasize the building's classical form, and its structural solidity, Berry added heavy pilasters of seasoned pine on each of the four exterior corners and on each side of the substantial double entrance door. The *pièce de résistance*, however, is the pediment, sup-

Government House, Fredericton as seen in 1880. The building was designed by J.E Woolford in the 1820s.

ported by Doric columns, which frames the royal coat of arms, hand-carved by a local ship's carpenter and painted in bright, heraldic colours. Unusually large, the carving and its uncompromising motto, *Dieu et Mon Droit*, fill the entire pediment. Inside the building, this show of loyalty is matched by portraits of the reigning queen, Queen Victoria, and commissioned photographs of the Gainsborough portraits of George III, his wife, Queen Charlotte, and 13 of their 15 children, now hanging in the Queen's Gallery at Windsor Castle.

For visiting English officials, buildings that would not have looked out of place in Cheltenham or Bath were reminders of the loyalty of their builders and of Britain's obligation to compensate them for the heavy price they had paid for it. If, as most Loyalists believed, they were victims of a "shameful peace," then there was a strong possibility that Britain might have been moved less by gratitude than guilt. It was important, therefore—guilt being the more perishable emotion—to remind Britain of their losses at every possible turn. When Prince Edward, the Duke of Kent, visited Saint John in 1794 Mayor Gabriel Ludlow was careful to point out that loyalty to his father (George III) had "induced [them] with cheerfulness to sacrifice the Comforts of [their] former situations, and seek an Asylum under the British constitution in this lately uncultivated wilderness." The message conveyed by a raw ten-year-old city perched on two rocky promontories could hardly have escaped the Prince but George Ludlow clearly felt that it would do no harm to enunciate it.

Public buildings with an explicitly British cast might have been effective reminders of Britain's obligation to the Loyalists, but they were expensive. Names, on the other hand, cost nothing and, had Prince Edward taken note of the street names in Saint John, he would have seen that he was in friendly, if not familiar, territory. In Loyalist towns it was standard practice to name the main streets King and Queen and the subsidiary streets after members of the royal family or faithful servants of the Crown. Thus in the old town plan of St. Andrews, 13 of the streets are named after the children of George III; the remainder are King—the show street—Queen, Prince of Wales, Carleton, and Parr. The only exception is Water Street, the name given, as in most coastal towns in the Bay of Fundy and the Gulf of Maine, to the street closest to the shore.

Churches

In Loyalist images of the ideal landscape, the indispensable ingredients were villages, manor houses, and attendant farms all cradled within an administrative framework of counties and parishes. For the devout, the image also needed the presence of the divine: the spire or tower of an established church. In the list of wants presented to the Colonial Office by the Loyalists of New Ireland, an ordained minister of the Church of England was second only to a constitution. As a Loyalist agent in Nova Scotia, Amos Botsford was charged with setting aside lands in each township for a school for learning the classics and a church for propagating the Anglican religion. "It is hoped," wrote his New York advisors, "that particular attention will be paid in preparing to build a Church, for which we have provided an Elegant Organ, and have a present of the Royal Arms embossed and blazoned in a very handsome manner." No less devout were the Connecticut/Long Island Loyalists at Kingston who, arriving in advance of the surveyors, set aside lands for a school, a church, and a rectory before choosing their farmlands.

For insecure refugees, faith and regular devotions were both a comfort and, by fending off barbarity and the wilderness, a shield. But for the planners of the settlement, and particularly for distant officials in the Colonial Office, the role of the Anglican church was less that of a shield against the wilderness without than a regulator for controlling the wilderness within. One of the lessons of the Revolution had been that religious dissent and political radicalism went hand in hand. Anglicanism may not have been a guarantee of loyalty but the most

The Charlotte County Courthouse, St Andrews.

Jamie Steel

Anglican of the colonies, New York, had also been the most loyal. The most rebellious, on the other hand, were the heavily Congregationalist New England colonies. New England Congregationalists insisted not only on the complete separation of church and state but on the independence of each congregation. Each was free to regulate its own business, decide on a method of worship, choose the liturgy, and appoint its own minister. Each church, in effect, was the ecclesiastical equivalent of the township.

In the still-loyal Maritime colonies, as in the rest of British North America, there would be no ambiguity about the role of the Church of England. It could bring hope and reassurance to the uncertain and the uprooted but at bottom it was to be an instrument of state. Through precept and example it would promote the monarchy, strengthen the principle of authority in government, and instill, through habits of deference and obedience, acceptance of hierarchy in society. By making no concessions to colonial conditions it held to the principle—an article of faith among colonial officials—that friction between the colonies and the mother country could virtually be eliminated by modelling all colonial institutions after those of the parent state. To "assimilate the Colony with the parent state," as John Simcoe, Governor of Upper Canada, put it, the "utmost attention should be paid [to] British Customs, Manners and Principles in the most trivial as well as serious matters." By any measure, the character and conduct of the colonial Church was a serious matter.

The most persistent exponent of a political role for the Church of England was the indefatigable William Knox, Under-Secretary at the American

The courthouse, Burton, New Brunswick, c.1900 (George Thomas Taylor).

Public Archives of New Brunswick

Department from 1770 to 1782. In a series of papers he argued that a soundly based Church of England was critical to the continuing support of the monarchy in the English-speaking colonies. Like other colonial officials, he must have hoped that in Nova Scotia the incoming Loyalists would raise the ecclesiastical balance in favour of the Church but he would also have known that in a colony that had been a haven for dissidents the weighting of the scales hardly favoured a reversal. Most of the New England Planters were Congregationalists and to these could be added Presbyterians from Scotland, Wesleyan Methodists from northern England, Catholics from the old Acadian settlements, Irish Catholics from Newfoundland, and Lutherans from Germany and Switzerland. Among the Loyalists themselves only the leaders were uniformly Anglican. A

A view of King's Square, Saint John, 1851. The paths of the square are laid out in the pattern of the Union Jack (John William Hill).

National Archives of Canada

church that valued decorum, ritual and a reasoned submission to law and order might not have appealed to all Loyalists, but for many these tenets made it a haven of civilized behaviour.

To make any headway in the remaining British colonies the Church of England would obviously need government encouragement and support. With only a handful of clergymen (New Brunswick had only six in 1785), few of whom were young and vigorous, it had no chance of meeting the needs of a pioneer society. To strengthen its position, the missionary wing of the Church, the government-funded Society for the Propagation of the Gospels Overseas

(SPG), concentrated almost exclusively on British North America after the loss of the American colonies. Africa and the Far East it ceded to the evangelicals and the dissidents. The SPG paid the stipends of the Anglican ministers and provided money and materials for church buildings.

In addition to financial aid, Knox also insisted on organizational support for the Church, in particular on the need for a resident bishop for Nova Scotia. A colonial bishop would replace the Bishop of London, the traditional overseer of the colonial church whose authority was tenuous at best, and ensure a sufficient supply of Anglican clergy. North American candidates for the ministry would no longer be discouraged by the expense and hazards of crossing the Atlantic for ordination. Knox also argued that as well as being financially independent of the laity the clergy should, like their English counterparts, operate within a clearly defined hierarchy headed, ultimately, by the monarch. A system of curates, vicars, canons, archdeacons, and deans overseen by a bishop would provide both a chain of authority and incentives for advancement. Knox was convinced that an episcopacy in the 13 colonies would have restrained the levelling, democratic opinions that, unchecked, had brought the Americans to open rebellion. With no episcopal control, Anglican practices were shot through with republican tendencies, individual congregations being nothing more than voluntary associations governed by elected wardens and a vestry.

The need for a firm Tory hand on the tiller of the Church in Nova Scotia was underlined by the competition for the rectorship of Christchurch, Shelburne. The candidates were Dr. William Walter, former rector of Trinity Church in Boston, and George Panton, former rector of a church in Trenton, New Jersey. Walter was the people's choice, resting his claim on his background and credentials and on "the Privilege and the Right of the Parishioners by Law to chuse their own minister." Panton, on the other hand, was a conservative and a member of the Fifty-five—and the choice of the SPG, the governor, and leading Loyalists. Walter accused Panton of being the candidate of privilege while Panton countered with charges of subversion, characterizing Walton as the embodiment of a "dangerous tendency" that would open doors to sectarian ideas threatening "to the Church and Government." He also confronted him with the general proposition that no "principled Loyalist" or "genuine member of the Church of England" would dare oppose established authority. But in a community suffering from what it perceived as government neglect and indifference, Panton's rallying cries of King and Country and respect for authority moved no one and he was denied the rectorship.

Viewed as a clash between the parishioners' right to choose and the obligation to support authority, the competition between the radical or Americanized

Dr Walter and the conservative George Panton was a prelude to the main ecclesiastical event of the 1780s—the competition for the position of bishop. Although contesting a larger prize on a larger stage, the two finalists, both Loyalist clergymen, came from the same camps as Walter and Panton. The people's choice, and the unanimous choice of the clergy of Nova Scotia and New Brunswick, was Samuel Peters, a New Englander and a former SPG missionary to Connecticut. Though a keen monarchist, he is said to have had very democratic ideas about the government of the colonial Church and was in favour of tailoring English institutions to fit colonial conditions. His rival, and the establishment's candidate, was Irish-born Charles Inglis, the decendant of several generations of ministers in the Scottish Episcopalian Church. As a young man Inglis had immigrated to Pennsylvania and worked his way through the ranks of the Anglican Church. Like Knox, Inglis associated dissent in religion with disloyalty in politics and is said to have believed that one of the objectives of the Revolution had been the overthrow of the Church of England. After the evacuation of New York in November 1783 he went to

Loyalist-built St. John's Kirk, 1805, Shelburne.

C.W. Jeffreys, Imperial Oil Collection

England in search of a comfortable living. Through his patron Lord Dorchester (the former Sir Guy Carleton) and his chief backer, the Bishop of London, Inglis's attention was directed instead to the see of Nova Scotia. In England, too, Inglis is said to have ingratiated himself with the Archbishops of Canterbury and York and to have won the support of the SPG whose general meetings he was careful to attend.

From London, where he had fled as a Loyalist refugee in 1776, Samuel Peters waged a pamphlet war against Inglis. Writing under the pseudonym "J. Viator," he denounced him as a wordly cleric who, as the holder of several lucrative military chaplaincies in New York, had spent more time lining his pockets than tending his flock. Inglis, too, had been one of the infamous Fifty-five. Peters was not alone in his denunciation. William Smith, former Chief Justice of New York, dismissed Inglis as "a Prigg Parson" while John Doty, a fellow clergyman, said he would serve as a Hackney parson "rather than submit to his [Inglis'] Lawn sleeves." Inglis's personal vanity, Doty claimed, would "bring on him the sneer and contempt of every honest and good man." Samuel Andrews, formerly of Connecticut and the first vicar of St. Andrews, thought that nothing could throw "a greater Damp" on the Church than to have Inglis ordained as the first bishop.

A sketch by J.E. Woolford, July 1817, showing Christ Church and Shelburne Harbour.

But neither Peters' pamphlets nor the obloquy of the colonial clergy had any effect on the British government or English ecclesiasts and in the autumn of 1787 Inglis became the first colonial bishop. As the champion of a centralized, pyramidally organized Church his appointment could hardly have been more timely. Nova Scotia and New Brunswick were then in the throes of an evangelical revival, a spillover from New England's Great Awakening, that threatened to engulf the traditional church. The chief herald of belief through revelation, as distinct from reason, was Henry Alline, a young Connecticut-born farmer who had come to Nova Scotia as part of the Planter migration of the 1760s. He urged the devout to read and interpret the Bible guided only by an "inner light," eschewing intermediaries. Practicing what he preached, at meetings he encouraged converted listeners to speak out, even to preach. Anglicans considered the practice dangerously "levelling."

To thorough converts to the faith, Alline also proffered the attractive doctrine that they could not sin in the spirit, a concession that a mischievious Colonel Gubbins took to mean that for New Lights there was no sin below the heart. By 1783, the New Light movement had swept through the Planter settlements in the Annapolis and Saint John Valleys carrying before it a weakened Congregationalist church. Isolated by the war from New England and unsupported by a missionary organization, it suffered from a chronic shortage of ministers. Following the collapse, moderate Congregationalists gravitated to the Presbyterians and Methodists, centrists and radicals to the Baptists. American-oriented, and wholly committed to the principles of local autonomy and control of the clergy by the laity, Baptism was the true heir of New England Congregationalism.

Rt. Rev. Charles Inglis D. D.

National Archives of Canada

Anglicans reacted to the evangelical onslaught with a chorus of invective, heavily freighted with images of pestilence and plague. Bishop Inglis reviled the "swarms of...ignorant, low and fanatical" teachers who "infest" every district and recoiled fom their "wild notionisms" delivered with "violent zeal [and] intrepidity of countenance." These were spread, like some deadly miasma, through "[a] great exertion of lungs." At Wilmot, where he was surrounded by Baptists and Methodists, John Wiswall complained of being assailed by "strolling, fanatical teachers" and their "deluded hearers." At Digby, Roger Viets was similarly beseiged, fighting to keep the town free of the "contagion" of Baptism, and at St. Andrews even the very moderate Samuel Andrews complained of a mission "infested" with "straggling New Lights" and "ignorant Anabaptist Teachers."

Where words failed to stem the dissident onslaught, Anglicans resorted to sticks and stones. Dissenting churches might be tolerated within the body politic but they need not be extended statutory rights. They received no government funds for ministers' salaries or church buildings and no rents or stumpage fees from glebe lands. Although Anglican glebe lands were not to exceed 1,000 acres and were, in the main, unproductive leftovers, the dissenting churches resented their very existence. Inglis also insisted that funds for building churches be withheld even from the Church of Scotland, the other official British church. He arranged for small grants for particular Presbyterian clergymen but he resisted all proposals to pay Presbyterian ministers from government funds. He also supported efforts to curtail the functions of the dissenting churches, helping to word New Brunswick's 1791 draconian Marriage Act. For the first third of the nineteenth century Methodist and Baptist clergymen in New Brunswick were forbidden, on pain of imprisonment, to perform marriage services; Quakers, Presbyterians, and Roman Catholic ministers could do so only when both parties were of the same faith. For dissidents the skies were no lighter in Nova Scotia. Marriages performed by licence, that is without the publication of marriage proclamations, came under the aegis of the Church of England. Licences, issued by Anglican ministers, were granted on condition that the ceremony conform to the rites and practices of the Church of England. Not until 1834 could dissident ministers get licences directly from the governor and conduct their own ceremonies, without restrictions. In New Brunswick, too, ministers' licences could be revoked if the holders were deemed a threat to public order. The act was seldom invoked but it gave the county magistrates who, like all important public oficials, were usually Anglican, considerable leverage.

Anglican intolerance of the dissenting churches contrasted sharply with what seems to have been the generally obliging disposition of the nonconformists toward the Church of England. Where they had no church of their own, Protestant dissenters often attended the services of the Church of England and, in the early years of settlement, they allowed its ministers to use their meeting houses. But Anglicans, on the whole, did not reciprocate, refusing to yield either in matters of funding or doctrine. By stubbornly insisting that all authority in church matters rested with the clergy, the church at St. Andrews lost its entire Presbyterian following. Content to share in Anglican services under the ministry of the tolerant Samuel Andrews, Presbyterians balked at the intransigence of his oligarchic successor who maintained that, in Church matters, complete authority rested in the clergy. The offending rector was eventually removed by the governor at the request of the vestry, and over the opposition of the bishop, but the removal was not in time to prevent the defection of the Presbyterians.

Anglicans also failed to adjust to the levelling effect of the frontier. In 1809, about a year before one of Bishop Inglis's infrequent sorties into his diocese, the congregation at Kingston, New Brunswick, had departed from the usual

Anglican procedure of "selling" or renting pews. Inglis was aghast at the move: "[It] gave me no small concern to learn that the pews in Kingston were all held in common, and that none were appropriated to individuals—as is the case in all other churches in our communion. I never knew an instance before this...where the pews were thus held in common, and where men—perhaps of the worst characters—might come and set themselves down by the most religious and respectable characters in the parish. This must ultimately tend to produce disorder and confusion in the church, and check the spirit of true devotion and piety." As obedient Anglicans, the parishioners voted overwhelmingly to comply with the bishop's wishes. The church returned to rented pews, continuing the practice until nearly every other rural parish in the diocese had abandoned it. Finally, in 1845, Bishop Medley decreed that "[all] the sittings be made *free*."

In Anglican churches, however, it was not only the poor who had to take a back seat. Although welcomed at church services and encouraged to take communion, Blacks were assigned to separate pews. At Gagetown, for example, there were separate pews for singers and for Blacks. On feast days and holidays, Blacks could find themselves without seats at all. To solve the problem of overcrowding on busy Sundays, John Breynton, rector of St. Paul's in Halifax, encouraged Blacks to meet in their homes where they were led by commissioned Black lay-readers. Among the readers was Joseph Leonard, a schoolteacher who, not content just to lead the services, administered communions, conducted baptisms and performed marriage services. Inglis was shocked but in spite of his reproval Leonard stood his ground, insisting that he wished to be ordained in the Church. But most Blacks, like most common folk, felt more comfortable with nonconformists and with the Wesleyan Methodists in particular. The Methodists opposed slavery, welcomed black members and did not segregate them. In 1790 one quarter of Nova Scotia's 800 Methodists were Black Loyalists.

But congregations divided, sometimes bitterly, because of the inflexibility of some Anglican clergy despite the presence of conditions that cried out for compromise. The most notorious incident occurred on Grand Manan. St. Paul's at Grand Harbour was built ostensibly to dispel the "appalling religious ignorance" that the Reverend Dr .Jerome Alley from St. Andrews—a noted conservative—had found there on a pastoral visit in 1820. It was expected that a building of the established church would not only remind the islanders of British sovereignty but might also help to stem the radical tide of Baptism then sweeping the island. But such was the egalitarian temper of early nineteenth-century Grand Manan (settled almost entirely by New Englanders), that even in the new Anglican Church, the altar—following New England Congregationalist tradition—was set among the congregation. In English churches the altar was always placed at the east end of the nave, distancing the clergy from their flocks.

The independence of the laity unsettled the first curate, an intemperate young Englishman, Cornelius Griffin, sent to the island by the SPG. "Each one," Griffin remarked of his parishioners, "thinks himself as much a king as the King of England." Careless, too, about regular times of worship they were clearly too proud "to be taught their Duty to God and man." Almost from its inception St. Paul's was riven by a feud between its first rector, John Dunn, said to have been "priggish about the dignity of his calling" and a powerful church warden, Wilfred Fisher, who was also a magistrate, the Commissioner of Roads, and Captain of the Militia. Unable to tolerate what he perceived as haughty indifference to the wardens and the vestry from a cleric half his age with no roots in the community, Fisher defected to the Baptists. Two years later, in 1839, he was charged with the deliberate firing of St. Paul's and the burning in effigy of its rector. After a month-long criminal trial in St. Andrews, at which 60 island men testified, Fisher and two other defendants were exonerated. St. Paul's was rebuilt, but with Grand Manan granite not wood.

As well as reviling sectarianism and denying government privileges to rival churches, leading Anglicans recognized that they should take positive steps to stem the evangelical tide. Fire, some suggested, should be fought with fire. Before the appointment of Charles Inglis, John Haliburton advised the SPG and government officials in London that a "small Tincture of Enthusiasm might not be Amiss" in the personality of the new bishop. As a critic of "lukewarmness" in the Anglican ministry, Inglis himself would have approved of the advice even though, as products of the European Enlightment, neither he nor his fellow clergy were capable of enthusiasm. By temperament and training they were committed to a decorous, heavily institutionalized brand of religion that placed reason before revelation, and ritual and decorum before the extemporaneous. In a context that called for inspiration and uplift the Anglicans could offer only cool rationalism. Furthermore, as ageing and, in some cases, infirm survivors of the Revolution their clergy were physically as well as temperamentally unable to play the role of missionaries in the wilderness. Most came from towns and cities and their ministries had been tailored to the needs of merchant and professional classes raised in the faith. With no feel for the tactics of conversion or the spiritual predilections of unlettered country people, in a race with the evangelical and dissident sects the Anglicans were non-starters.

Church Buildings

Unable or unwilling to summon up enthusiasm, or modify its rituals, the Church of England turned outward, concentrating on building programmes and the government of the Church. Whereas a plain meeting house might have satisfied the dissident sects, Anglicans considered a consecrated church essential to their form of worship. On his arrival in Nova Scotia, Charles Inglis was disturbed by the shortage of provincial churches and shocked by their condition. The log-built church at Windsor, originally designed as a schoolhouse, he considered a "wretched hovel." Only St. Paul's in Halifax, built in 1750, met with his approval. Even the usually complaisant Governor Parr was dismayed. In contrast to the "well-built" dissenting churches, which were "finished with full congregations," the Anglican churches, railed the governor, were "unfinished, miserable looking, and nearly deserted."

The initiative for church building came from the bishop and William Morice, Secretary of the SPG. Inglis's first tour of the major settlements, in 1788, convinced him that the older settlements needed as much help as the new. Even where there was no need for a new church the existing one inevitably needed refurbishing and repair. But neither the British Government nor the SPG were sympathetic to his views. Older settlements were persistently denied funds, the available money going to Loyalist settlements such as Shelburne, Digby, and Guysborough. The Cornwallis churchwarden, John Burbridge, objected to the exclusion of the older settlements which, like Inglis, he believed to be in just as much need as the new. But of the older settlements only Granville and Annapolis received a share of the parliamentary grant.

To prevent the mishandling of funds and delays in building, payments were made in three installments: the first when work began, the second when the building was half completed, and the third when it was finished. No payment came from England without a certificate from the bishop. Inglis considered that building was underway after the signing of a *bona fide* contract with qualified workmen; half finished when the frame was boarded in and the roof shingled; and completely finished when the inside walls had been plastered, window glass and doors fitted, and the pews built.

Because of the general shortage of money and materials, Anglican churches built during the early period were of simple design, usually a box-like body capped by a sloping roof and a bell tower or steeple. All were built of wood, stone being too costly. The buildings were generally small; however, if enough money was available, they included a second storey to provide pews or a gallery for the poor, for Blacks, and—in garrison towns—for common soldiers. The smaller churches were built to accommodate two or three hundred people but the larger ones, as at Shelburne, could seat up to a thousand.

Although a promoter of church building, Inglis was distressed when, as in Fredericton, scale and costs got out of hand. In choosing Portland Chapel, London, as the model for their church he thought the Fredericton Loyalists had gone too far. Work on Christ Church began in 1788 but because ambition outran resources work had to be abandoned after about a year. Work resumed in 1791 but progress was slow and the pews were not installed until 1794. By 1798 the building was still not completely finished. Inglis was equally put out by John Wiswall's preoccupation with the construction of Old Holy Trinity Church at Wilmot. Wiswall, who was not noted for missionary zeal, was rebuked by Inglis for neglecting the rest of his parish; at Aylesford he had preached only one sermon in eight weeks. Inglis's favourite church, "the neatest, best finished church in the province," was St. Mary's, Auburn. A century after its completion the weather vane blew down cracking open a ball that proved to be a time capsule. Inside were documents providing details of methods of construction and the building materials used. Framing, boards, and shingles were of local pine but doors, window frames and rails were brought from Halifax. Nails, too, came from the city—packed in 10- or 15-pound lots, they were carried by soldiers along the 100-mile long military road from Halifax to Auburn. The timber framing was nailed together on the ground and raised with iron-pointed pike poles.

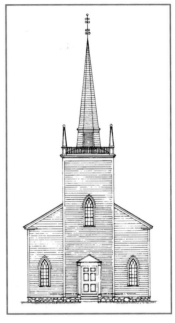

Holy Trinity Church, Wilmot, Nova Scotia.

Whatever angst the construction programme may have given the bishop, churches were one of the most distinctive features of the Loyalist settlement. With connections to both the old world and the new, the Loyalists were able to marry the plain, sometimes steeple-less American meeting house with the dashing British classical church. The result of the union was a church architecture unique to the Maritimes. From the meeting house came the simple rectangular form, sturdy construction, the sheath of narrow clapboarding and the pitched roof. But the details—pediments, capitals, Palladian windows, and Wren-like steeples—were a gift of British classicism. But however appealing the product, subsidized construction was not without disadvantages. Government grants are thought to have so undermined local initiative that except for the church at Kingston no other Anglican church was built by the settlers themselves. As a result, Anglican congregations seldom developed the sense of community that came from building a church and a manse and supporting a local minister.

St Mary's Anglican Church, Auburn, Nova Scotia, built in 1790.

Public Archives of Nova Scotia

Schools and Colleges

Without a nursery to prepare candidates for the ministry, Knox realized that his plans for the colonial Church would never be realized and his efforts to install a colonial bishop largely wasted. He therefore urged the formation of grammar schools, offering Greek and Latin, that would prepare youths for college and, ultimately, public office and the Church. In the absence of a college he feared a drift to the United States where the students were bound to imbibe principles unfriendly to the British constitution. On his accession in Nova Scotia, Charles Inglis took up Knox's refrain, seeing a college chiefly as a means of guaranteeing a supply of candidates for Holy Orders and ending reliance on Britain.

Because there could be no college without matriculants from a grammar school, attention at first focused on the latter. To shield students from the temptations of the city, Charles Inglis and Alexander Croke, a future governor, recommended a location outside Halifax. Still cherished was the classical ideal of a rural or suburban school where, as Croke put it, "students emboldened by the grape" would be safe from "venal nymphs and their painted charms" who were ever ready to "lure the novice to their hackneyed arms." For Charles Inglis, with his farming and horticultural interests, there were less prurient reasons for a rural location. He suggested that about 100 acres be set aside for teaching agriculture and botany, arguing—with the object of promoting agriculture in boreal places—that such studies had been of great service to Sweden.

In 1788 the provincial assembly granted funds for the rent of a building in Windsor to house a fee-paying school and the support of a master for one year. The following year the Assembly went farther, passing an act to establish a college and voting money for the purchase of land on which to build both a grammar school and a college. Royal approval, accompanied by a substantial grant toward the building programme, followed in 1790. But because of the expense of building and the difficulty of attracting teachers, King's College grew slowly, allowing a Methodist minister, Joshua Marsden, to comment in 1800 that it contributed little either to learning or to piety. A substantial grant from the Colonial Office in 1802 eased the financial burden but it did little for learning or piety. In 1815, Henry Bliss wrote to his friend Neville Parker:

"We have been as gay in Windsor as you have been in Saint John; not that we have had any very agreeable parties, but Inglis has much better wine than usual, and it has been poured down pretty freely....The term commenced with a great run of gaming. Monk, about a week ago, had lost twenty pounds. Yesterday he owed J. Uniake eight pounds, but last night he reduced the whole, and ran up again to four. I have won a little. J. Uniake, at one time, had won upwards of twelve pounds. I have seen Master Lud play very high, from morning to night. They used to play all Sunday, in Monk's room. Monk even carried a pack of cards, wherever he went, in his pocket, and played [during] prayers, and dinner. I played one day from morning to night, and ... I won that day four pounds five. Ned Monk one day, on getting up from the table, said very indifferently, 'I've lost more than I can ever pay.' The rural location, clearly, had not worked.

Yet libertarianism at King's did not extend beyond matters of conduct. The statutes of the College, drawn up by Charles Inglis and two other governors, required all matriculants to subscribe to the Thirty-nine Articles of the Church of England, effectively closing the college to dissenters. Inglis also insisted that to prevent the college from becoming "a seminary for Dissenters" at least two of the professorships and the office of the president should be restricted to Church of England clergymen.

The effect of the embargo was the immediate alienation of the Presbyterians, the largest single denomination in the province, and the ultimate alienation of all the dissenting churches once these decided to erase publicly the Anglican-applied stigma of ignorance and illiteracy. In 1811, Thomas McCulloch, the headmaster of the Presbyterian-administered Pictou school presented a plan for converting it into an interdenominational college, modelled on the liberal principles of the Scottish universities. But only faint support from the Baptists and

King's College, Windsor.

Methodists, and strong resistance from the Anglican council and the equally exclusionist Church of Scotland, put paid to any hope of interdenominational higher education in Nova Scotia. There was also opposition to the scheme from Governor Dalhousie who was attempting to establish a non-sectarian college of his own in Halifax. Dalhousie's model was Edinburgh University, which had no religious affiliations, but all his governors were either Anglican or Presbyterian, several of the former already serving on the board of King's College. A draft plan to unite the two colleges, in 1823, pleased neither Anglicans or Presbyterians, the rambunctious King's students refusing to have any truck with the "scotch bastard of a University." Ecumenical failure led, inevitably, to a proliferation of colleges so that by the end of the century Nova Scotia, for its size and population, had more colleges than any other province in Canada: King's (1802)–Anglican; Pictou Academy (1805)–Presbyterian but open to all; Dalhousie (1818)–non sectarian; Acadia (1838)–Baptist; St. Mary's (1841), St. Francis Xavier (1853), and Université Sainte-Anne (1890)–Roman Catholic.

In New Brunswick, with its vaulting ambition to be a gentlemanly province, there was a greater emphasis on a secular role for education. But here, as in Nova Scotia, the leading Loyalists were unwilling or unable to do much beyond their own class. Determined to protect their children from the coarsening effects

King's College, Windsor, 1803, from a drawing by the Reverend Benjamin Gerrish Gray.

of the frontier, they chanelled scarce educational funds into schooling for an elite. In 1793 the Executive Council blocked an early attempt by the Assembly to establish a parish school system, leaving the education of the common folk to the Church and enterprising or philanthropic individuals. In 1785 the Council approved a charter for a provincial college but the British government, uncertain of its educational plans for the provinces, refused to grant articles of incorporation. By 1790, with the endownment of King's College on the understanding that it would serve students from all the North American colonies, it was

*The Collegiate School and Christ Church, Fredericton, c. 1835. Barely visible
on the far left of the painting, amongst the foliage on the hill, is the outline of*

King's College which opened in 1829. Because of damage to the painting, part of the structure is no longer visible (George Neilson Smith).

The Beaverbrook Art Gallery, Fredericton, New Brunswick

clear that Britain would not underwrite a second North American college. George Leonard, for whom a classical education was as central to the Loyalist cause as the Navigation Laws and the Anglican Church, tried without success to find private English patrons for an academy and a provincial library. With no overseas support, all that New Brunswick could manage before 1800 was a grammar or preparatory school in Fredericton supported in part by a generous land grant. Both teachers and students, without exception, were Anglican.

The absence of a provincial college left prominent New Brunswick Loyalists with no choice but to send their sons to King's or, if they could afford to do so, to Harvard or Yale and, for law, to London's Inns of Court. With the eligible young men away, perhaps never to return, the province's well-to-do young women were faced with the daunting prospect of marrying, as George Leonard put it, "the common peasantry of the country." The approval, in 1800, of a charter for the College of New Brunswick relieved that anxiety but the relief was not immediate. Not until 1820 could the college afford a president and it was not officially opened, as King's College, until 1829. A new college called for a new building and one was built, by John Elliott Woolford, on a slope overlooking Fredericton. The faculty, but not the students, had to be Anglican. Against strong ecclesiastical opposition, its new president, Sir Howard Douglas, insisted that in a province with such a large nonconformist element, religious tests and subscription to the Thirty-nine Articles be applied only to students of divinity. Yet because of its allegedly narrow classical course of instruction and its ties to the Church of England, the college was unpopular with both the people and the provincial assembly. The slackening of its religious affiliation and its 1854 re-chartering as the University of New Brunswick brought it closer to the people; however, as Esther Clark Wright pointed out, it took a Baptist professor of Mathematics, without connections to the Loyalist elite, to bring the college closer to the mainstream of provincial life—first as chancellor, then as president. A chair of civil engineering and surveying was added in 1889 and a school of forestry, the first in Canada, in 1907.

The Loyalist Imprint

W hen measured against the ideal of New Ireland, the Loyalist achievement in New Brunswick and Nova Scotia fell short of expectations.
A wilderness had been settled and subdued but, defeated by the
reductionism of the frontier and Britain's refusal to underwrite a colonial aristocracy, the leaders of the settlement failed to achieve their dream of a layered,
socially unified society. By turning their backs on the Church of England the
Loyalist rank-and-file rejected not just the established church but the social and
political ideals on which it rested. They remained loyal to the Crown but not in
the deferential ways their leaders would have wished. Prosperity also eluded
the Loyalist settlement. Not only were the provinces unable to produce surpluses large enough to satisfy West Indian and British demands but for much of the
time they were reduced to carrying American produce. Without the protective
umbrella of the Navigation Acts and favoured treatment for colonial goods in
British ports (the colonial preference), the provinces were no match for New
England and the seaboard states. The Maritimes were not unimportant to
Britain but the needs of other colonies, such as the West Indies, took priority.
"The original connexions and attachments," Benjamin Marston noted as early
as 1790, "are long since worn out." The gamble with Britain and the Atlantic
trade had failed and the provinces were in a poor position, both geographically
and psychologically, to face about and embrace the continent.

The Loyalists also misjudged the political stability and the economic potential of the new American states. When visiting Massachusetts in 1799 Edward
Winslow found a touching civility, not the chaos and anarchy he and others
had predicted 15 years earlier. Prosperity, too, was general but, unable to
admit that it was soundly based, he attributed it—without much conviction—

to the windfall of the Napoleonic wars. Far from being the envy of the American States and syphoning Americans northward, the Maritimes were a drain for returnees to New England and the eastern seaboard. For discontented refugees, the cutting-off of government provisions in 1787 removed a major incentive to stay, and for military personnel drawing pensions and half-pay, the waiving of the imperial residence requirement meant that there was then no necessity to do so. Tradesmen and suppliers in any way dependent on army pensioners were similarly unsettled. Nova Scotia, which suffered by far the largest exodus, may have lost as much as half of its Loyalist population. As previously mentioned, the outflow was so great that in 1789 the Provincial Assembly passed an act preventing people leaving the province without a pass. Some of the escapees chose to remain under the British flag by going to Ontario, Britain, and the Bahamas but most returned to the United States. Greatly outnumbered by the old inhabitants and incoming Scots, Irish, and English, within a few years the Nova Scotia Loyalists ceased to exist as an identifiable group.

In New Brunswick, where there was no large resident population to contend with, and no urban disasters on the scale of Shelburne, losses were far lighter. Only about 15 percent of the Loyalists left the province and the remaining 85 percent were undisturbed by new immigrants until the close of the Napoleonic Wars. But once immigration resumed they, too, were quickly outnumbered. Between 1825-1850, the population of New Brunswick increased from just under 75,000 to almost 194,000. By 1851, 40 per cent of the people in Charlotte County, one of the most Loyalist of New Brunswick's counties, were from Ireland, 6 per cent from Scotland, 3 per cent from England and 6 per cent from the United States. Of the 44 per cent born in New Brunswick, a majority were the children of post-Napoleonic War British immigrants. For New Brunswick as a whole, probably not more than a third of the people born in the province, that is, 15 per cent of the total population, were Loyalist or of Loyalist descent.

Whether the measure is population, economics, or culture, the Loyalist ascendancy in the Maritimes was short-lived. But as the largest and most assertive of early immigrant groups, the Loyalists left an indelible mark. In New Brunswick, the administrative network of counties and, formerly, of parishes was largely theirs, as were—in both provinces—many of the town plans and rural surveys. Names with royal or British associations abound, and one still sees an occasional Union Jack raised defiantly against republicans on both sides of the border. Buildings, too, have survived and, in the case of St. Andrews and Shelburne, parts of two entire towns. Bypassed by the main flows of nineteenth-century commerce and trade, both were, as preservationists would see it, spared dynamic growth. Only remnants of Shelburne have sur-vived, but St. Andrews—whose decline was neither as swift nor as complete—has a larger number of surviving buildings. The older parts of Fredericton are also well preserved; as a garrison, a government; and then a university city, its growth was measured, and as the provincial capital it has always been conscious of the need to preserve something of its past.

Of the major Loyalist foundations, the most damaged was Saint John. A suc-cession of fires beginning in 1837 and culminating in the great fire of 1877 oblit-erated the Loyalist landscape. All that remains of the old city is the courthouse, a handful of houses, a burying ground, the outlines of King and Queen squares, and the original street plan. Yet in spite of such meagre pickings, Saint John still calls itself the Loyalist City, and this appellation, against all logic, remains valid. What matters in Saint John, as elsewhere in the Loyalist world, is not the quantity of the survivals but their quality, or rather their *character*. In matters of

Saint John Harbour c. 1827.

Nova Scotia Museum

design—whether of towns, buildings, furniture, or glassware—the Georgians, as John Gloag remarked, never seemed to put a foot wrong. Guided by classical rules of harmony, scale, and proportion, their artifacts were always finely made, restrained and, in the case of buildings, symmetrical, well-proportioned, and of human scale. The Georgian world, in Gloag's phrase, was one of splendid orderliness. For a century and more, the North American colonies constituted a community of taste guided by classical rules. Ideas about what constituted good or adequate design were generally agreed-upon. In drawings that were part of the contract specifications for buildings, the architect or designer could often ignore finishing details, confident that each master builder or joiner could be relied on to produce his own pattern within carefully-understood limits of taste.

For subsequent architects and designers, however, and critics such as John Ruskin, classical principles of harmony and proportion were an intolerable strait-jacket that inhibited invention and the use of new building methods and materials. Therefore, they and later generations broke the Georgian mold. Since Victorian times, there have been few rules and little consistency. For a public faced with an often-bewildering medley of architectural styles, Georgian certainties are a relief. In old Maritime or New England churchyards, it is these thin, graceful stones with their restrained Roman numerals, rather than the attention-seeking Victorian and Edwardian monuments, that tend to catch the eye and set the tone of the place. In the same way, a street, or even an entire town, can take its character from a handful of classical buildings. Because each building is a repetition of basic forms and proportions, it is not difficult to reconstruct the whole. In a well-preserved Georgian street or square, both eye and spirit can relax; there will be no jarring surprises nor, on the other side of the coin, exhilarating ones either. For the Loyalists, Georgian design and building brought relief from a natural wilderness; for moderns, from a wilderness of our own making.

Sources and further reading

General History

Brown, Wallace, *Victorious in Defeat: the American Loyalists in Exile* (New York, 1984).

Buckner, Philip A. and Reid, John G. eds., *The Atlantic Region to Confederation* (Toronto, 1994).

Condon, Ann Gorman, *The Envy of the American States: the Loyalist Dream for New Brunswick*.

MacKinnon, Neil, *This Unfriendly Soil: the Loyalist Experience in Nova Scotia 1783-1791* (Kingston and Montreal, 1986).

Moore, Christopher, *The Loyalists: Revolution, Exile, Settlement* (Toronto, 1984).

MacNutt, W.S. *New Brunswick, a History:1784-1867* (Toronto, 1963).

MacNutt, W.S., *The Atlantic Provinces: The Emergence of a Colonial Society* (Toronto, 1965).

Upton, L.F.S., *The United Empire Loyalists, Men and Myths* (Toronto, 1967).

Wright, Esther Clark, *The Loyalists of New Brunswick* (Fredericton, 1955).

Particular History

The Loyalist Blueprint

Bellot, Leland J., William Knox, The Life and Thought of an Eighteenth-century Imperialist (Austin, 1977).

Ells, Margaret, "Loyalist Attitudes," *Dalhousie Review*, Vol.15, Oct. 1935, 321-334.

Siefert, W.H., "The Exodus of the Loyalists from Penobscot and the Loyalist Settlements at Passamaquoddy," *Coll. New Brunswick Historical Society*, 3, 9, 1914, 485-529.

Williamson, Joseph, "The Proposed Province of New Ireland." *Coll. Maine Historical Society*, Series 1, Vol. 7, 1876, 201-211.

Williamson, Joseph, "The British Occupation of Penobscot," *Coll. Maine Historical Society*, Series 2, Vol.1, 1890, 392-400.

The New Land

Aiton, Grace, *The Story of Sussex and Vicinity* (Kingston, 1967).

Allen, Robert S., *The Loyal Americans: The Military Role of the Loyalist Provincial Corps and Their Settlement in British North America, 1775-1784.* (Ottawa, 1983).

Bird, J. Brian, "Settlement Patterns in Maritime Canada, 1687-1786," *Geographical Review*, 45, 3, 1955, 384-404.

Bumsted, J.M., "The Origin of the Land Question in Prince Edward Island, 1767-1805," *Acadiensis*, 9,1, 1981, 43-56.

Calneck, W.A., *History of the County of Annapolis* (Toronto, 1897).

Cameron, Ella Hunt, "Imperial Policy in Cape Breton, 1784-1795," *Coll. Nova Scotia Historical Society*, Vol. 31, 1957, 38-49.

Campbell, Patrick, *Travels in the Interior Inhabited parts of North America in the years 1791 and 1792* (rep. Toronto, 1937).

Chard, Donald F., "Charles Morris, 1731-1802," *Dictionary of Canadian Biography*, V, 607-608.

Coffin, Captain Henry, *A Memoir of General John Coffin* (Reading, 1880).

Condon, Ann Gorman, "George Leonard, 1742-1826," *Dictionary of Canadian Biography*, VI, 394-396.

Condon, Ann Gorman, "Edward Winslow, 1746/7-1815," *Dictionary of Canadian Biography*, VI, 865-868

Crathorne, Ethel, "The Morris family—surveyors general," *Nova Scotia Historical Quarterly*, Vol. 6, 1976, 207-216.

Cuthbertson, Brian, *A Biography of Richard John Uniacke, 1753-1830* (Halifax, 1980).

Eberlein, Harold D., *The Manors and Historic Homes of the Hudson Valley* (Philadelphia, 1924).

Fellows, Robert, "George Sproule," *Dictionary of Canadian Biography*, V, 773-774.

Fellows, Robert, "The Loyalists and Land Settlement in New Brunswick, 1783-1790," *Canadian Archivist*, 2,2, 1971, 5-15.

Fisher, Peter, *The First History of New Brunswick* (1825, rep. Woodstock, 1980).

Godfrey, W.G. "Thomas Carleton,1735-1817," *Dictionary of Canadian Biography*, V, 155-162.

Hodges, Graham R., *The Black Loyalist Directory* (New York, 1996).

Labaree, Leonard ed., *Royal Instructions to British Colonial Governors 1670-1776*, New York, 1935.

Longley, R.S., "An Annapolis County Loyalist," *Coll. Nova Scotia Historical Society*, Vol. 31, 1957, 73-95.

Maxwell, L.M.B., *An Outline of the History of Central New Brunswick* (Sackville, 1937).

Morgan, Robert J., "The Loyalists of Cape Breton," *Dalhousie Review*, 55, 2, 1975, 5-15.

McManis, Douglas R., *Colonial New England* (New York: 1975)

Nashwaak Bicentennial Association, *And the River Rolled On: Two Hundred Years on the Nashwaak*, 1984.

Raddall, Thomas H., "Tarleton's Legion," *Coll. Nova Scotia Historical Society*, Vol. 28, 1949, 1-41.

Raymond, W.O., *The River St. John* (Sackville, 1910)

Raymond, W.O., *The Winslow Papers AD 1776-1826* (Boston, 1972).

Spray, W.A., "Stair Agnew, 1757-1821," *Dictionary of Canadian Biography*, VI, 6-7.

Spray, W.A. "John Saunders, 1754-1834," *Dictionary of Canadian Biography*, VI, 683-687.

Temperley, Howard ed., *New Brunswick Journals of Lieutenant Colonel Joseph Gubbins, 1811 & 1813* (Fredericton, 1980).

Temperley, Howard, "Frontierism, Capital, and the American Loyalists in Canada," *Journal of American Studies*, 13, 1979, 5-27.

Thomson, Don W., *Men and Meridians: The History of Surveying and Mapping in Canada*, Vol. 1 (Ottawa, 1966).

Walker, James W. *The Black Loyalists: The Search for the Promised Land in Nova Scotia and Sierra Leone, 1783-1870* (New York, 1976).

Wynn, Graeme, "Population Patterns in Pre-Confederation New Brunswick," *Acadiensis*, 10, 1, 1981, 125-131.

Wynn, Graeme, "Late Eighteenth-Century Agriculture on the Bay of Fundy Marshlands," *Acadiensis*, 8, 2, 1979, 80-89.

Young, D.M., "Dugald Campbell,1758-1810" *Dictionary of Canadian Biography*, V, 135-137.

Young, D.M., "Beamsley Glasier,1714-1784," *Dictionary of Canadian Biography*, IV, 300-301.

Zuckermann, Michael, *Peacable Kingdoms: New England Towns in the Eighteenth Century* (New York, 1978).

Building The Towns

Banks, William Nathaniel, "Castine, Maine, and St Andrews, New Brunswick, Canada," *Antiques*, July 1980, 109-119.

Bates, Walter, *Kingston and the Loyalists of the "Spring Fleet" of 1783* (rep. Fredericton, 1980).

Bell, David G., *Early Loyalist Saint John* (Fredericton, 1983).

Calder, Doris, *All Our Born Days* (Sackville, 1984).

Collie, Michael, *New Brunswick* (Toronto, 1974).

Condon, Ann Gorman, "Loyalist Style and the Culture of the Atlantic Seaboard," *Material History Bulletin*, 25, Spring 1987, 22-27.

Ennals, Peter and Holdsworth, Deryck, "Vernacular Architecture and the Cultural Landscape of the Maritime Provinces - a Reconnaissance," *Acadiensis* 10, 2, 1981, 86-106.

Ennals, Peter, "The Yankee Origins of Bluenose Vernacular Architecture," *American Review of Canadian Studies*, 12, 2, 1982, 86-106.

Holmes, Theodore C., *Loyalists to Canada, the Quakers of Pennfield* (Camden, 1992).

Haliburton, Thomas C., *Nova Scotia* (1829).

Hugo-Brunt, Michael, "The Origin of Colonial Settlements in the Maritimes," *Plan Canada*, 1, 2, 1960, 78-144.

Jost, A.C., *Guysborough Sketches and Other Essays* (Kentville, 1950).

Mekeel, Arthur J., "The Quaker-Loyalist Migration to New Brunswick and Nova Scotia in 1783," *Bull. Friends Historical Association*, Vol. 32, Autumn 1943, 65-74.

Morgan, R.J., "Joseph Frederick Wallet DesBarres, 1721-1824" *Dictionary of Canadian Biography*, VI, 192-197.

Raymond, W.O., "The Founding of Shelburne. Benjamin Marston at Halifax, Shelburne and Mirimachi," *Coll. New Brunswick Historical Society*, No. 8, 1909, 204-277.

Robertson, Marion, *Kings Bounty: A History of Early Shelburne*, (Halifax:1983).

Schuyler, George W., *A City in the Wilderness* (Saint John, 1984).

Smith, Stuart, "Architecture in New Brunswick," *Canadian Antiques Collector*, May/June 1975, 37-42.

Smith, T. Watson, "The Loyalists at Shelburne," *Coll. Nova Scotia Historical Society*, Vol. 6, 1888, 53-89.

Squires, W. Austin, *A History of Fredericton* (Fredericton, 1980).

Stelter, Gilbert A., "The Classical Ideal, Cultural and Urban Form in Eighteenth-century Britain and America," *Journal of Urban History*, 10, 4, 1984, 351-382.

Wood, J.D. "Grand Design on the Fringes of Empire: New Towns for British North America," *Canadian Geographer* 26, 3, 1982, 243-255.

Wright, Esther Clark, *The St. John River and its Tributaries* (Toronto, 1949).

Public and Official Buildings

Cuthberston, Brian, *The First Bishop* (Halifax, 1987).

Duffus, Allan et al., *Thy Dwellings Fair: Churches of Nova Scotia, 1750-1830* (Hantsport, 1982).

Fingard, Judith, *The Anglican Design in Loyalist Nova Scotia*

(London, 1972).

Gloag, John, *Georgian Grace* (London, 1956).

Gowans, Alan, *Building Canada: An Architectural History of Canadian Life* (Toronto, 1966).

Gowans, Alan, *Looking at Architecture in Canada* (Toronto, 1958).

Hughes, Gary, *Music of the Eye: Architectural Drawings of Canada's First City, 1822-1914* (Saint John, 1992).

Kalman, Harold, *A History of Canadian Architecture* (Toronto, 1994).

McBeath, George, *New Brunswick's Old Government House* (Fredericton, 1995).

Pacey, Elizabeth, *Landmarks* (Halifax, 1994).

Robertson, Marion, "Isaac Hildreth: Loyalist Architect," *The Coastguard*, July 8, 1965, 26-28.

Unpublished Sources

Theses

Acheson, T.W., 'Denominationalism in a Loyalist county: a social history of Charlotte, 1783-1940' (University of New Brunswick M.A. thesis, 1964).

Conrad, Harold E., "The Loyalist experiment in New Brunswick" (Univ. of Toronto Ph.D. thesis, 1934).

Duval, Carle, "Edward Winslow, Portrait of a Loyalist" (Univ. of New Brunswick M.A. thesis, 1960).

Gilroy, Marion E., "The Loyalist Experiment in New Brunswick" (Univ. of New Brunswick M.A. thesis, 1933).

MacKinnon, Neil, "The Loyalist experience in Nova Scotia," 1783 to 1791 (Queen's Univ., Ph.D thesis, 1975).

Milton, Lorna Elizabeth, "Three Generations of Loyalist Gentlemen: The Botsford Men of Westmorland County" (Mount Allison University B.A. thesis, 1981).

Moore, Diana Ruth, "John Saunders 1754-1834: Consummate Loyalist" (Univ. of New Brunswick M.A. thesis, 1980).

Nason, Roger, "'Meritorious but Distressed Individuals,' the Penobscot Loyalist association and the settlement of the township of St Andrews" (Univ. of New Brunswick M.A. thesis, 1985).

Pilon, Beatrice, "The Settlement and Early Development of the Parish of Kingsclear, York County, 1784-1840" (Univ. of New Brunswick M.A. thesis, 1966).

Propokow, Michael John, "A True and Accurate Apprisement: Inequality in the Probate Wealth of Loyalist Charlotte and Kings Counties 1785-1820' (Univ. of New Brunswick M.A. thesis, 1985).

Purdy, Judson, "The Church of England in New Brunswick During the Colonial Era," (Univ. of New Brunswick M.A. thesis, 1954).

Showers, Violet Mary-Ann, "The Price of Loyalty, The Case of Benjamin Marston" (Univ. of New Brunswick M.A. thesis, 1982).

Sloan, Robert Wesley, "Loyalists in Eastern Maine During the American Revolution," (Univ. of Michigan Ph.D. thesis, 1971).

Snowdon, James Dean, "Footprints in the Marsh Mud: Politics and Land Settlement in the Township of Sackville 1760-1800"(Univ. of New Brunswick M.A. thesis, 1976)

Troxler, Carole W., "Migration of Carolina and Georgia Loyalists to Nova Scotia and New Brunswick" (Univ. of North Carolina Ph.D. thesis, 1974).

Watson, Raymond G., "Local Government in a New Brunswick County, King's County 1784-1850" (Univ. of New Brunswick M.A. thesis, 1969).

Manuscripts

Bliss, H., King's College, letter to Neville Parker, 15 June, 1815, Mowat Coll., Charlotte Co. Archives, New Brunswick.

Harvey, D.C., "The New England Township in Nova Scotia,"(Dalhousie Univ. Pam. Box J6).

Morris, John Spry, "General Instructions to Deputy Surveyors, 1839," Public Archives of Nova Scotia.

Morse, Robert, "Report on Nova Scotia, 1784," Public Archives of Nova Scotia.

Perley, Israel, "Survey book 1787-1803," Ganong Coll., New Brunswick Museum.

Sproule, George, "Letterbooks 1785-1789," Records of the Surveyors General, Public Archives of New Brunswick.

Williamson, Marcia, "The Coffin Houses," New Brunswick Museum, 1974.

Index

Mi'kmaq: 11, 12, 13

Minas Basin: 34

Monkton: 30

Morris, Charles: 17, 18, 34, 58, 64, 68, 76

Morris, William: 67, 69, 70, 71, 72,

Morristown: 68

Morse, Colonel Robert: 77, 78, 97

Morton, Nancy: 30

N

Napoleanic War: 23, 36, 92, 132

Nashwaak: 19, 44, 48, 51

New Brunswick Agricultural & Emigrant Society: 21

New Brunswick: 1, 8, 10, 11, 16, 17, 20, 21, 23, 26, 27, 30, 32, 33, 39, 48, 49, 50, 51, 54, 55, 56, 60, 67, 69, 76, 84, 91,

New England Planters: 12, 34, 35, 39, 56, 58, 60, 63, 78, 114, 117

New England: 5, 10, 13, 30, 33, 34, 35, 36, 39, 40, 46, 47, 54, 55, 56, 57, 58, 62, 63, 66, 78, 87, 88, 95, 96, 112, 117, 118, 120, 121, 131, 132, 134

New Hampshire: 17

New Haven: 33

New Ireland: 2, 3, 4, 5, 9, 111, 131

New Manchester: 46

New Scotland: 2

New York: vi, 2, 7, 13, 14, 15, 35, 36, 47, 49, 61, 67, 68, 72, 74, 76, 79, 112, 116, 117

Newfoundland: 95, 96, 114

Newton: 61

Norris, William: 68

North America: 1, 8, 79, 82, 88

North Carolina: 54

North, Lord: 5

Northumberland Strait: 11

Norton: 33

Nova Scotia: 1, 2, 4, 7, 8, 9, 10, 11, 15, 16, 17, 32, 33, 34, 36, 37, 39, 46, 47, 49, 50, 51, 52, 54, 56, 57, 58, 60, 61, 63, 67, 72, 64, 68, 69, 72, 73, 79, 93, 96, 97, 106, 111, 114, 115, 116, 117, 119, 120, 123, 124, 126, 131, 132

Nova Scotia Assembly: 93

O

Old Firth House, Shelburne: 90

Old Holy Trinity Church, Wilmot: 123

Ontario: 7, 50, 132

P

Panton, George: 115, 116

Parr, Governor John: 8, 14, 15, 33, 34, 35, 47, 51, 52, 68, 71, 78, 79, 90, 91, 105, 122

Parrtown: 74, 76

Passamaquaddy Bay: 10, 11, 12, 49, 55, 67

Patriots: 6

Penn, William: 65

Pennfield Ridge: 67

Pennsylvania: 67, 116

Penobscot Association: 66

Penobscot River: 2, 3, 5

Peters, Samuel: 116

Peters, Thomas: 54, 117

Peticodiac: 55

Philadelphia: 2, 65, 79

Planters: *see* New England Planters

Port Mouton: 47, 67

Port Roseway Associates: 68, 69

Port Roseway: 68, 69, 71, 90

Portland Chapel: 123

Portland: 3

Prince Edward Island: 7, 14, 32, 44, 63, 77, 97

Prince Edward the Duke of Kent: 111

Prince of Wales Street: 111

Prince William: 21

Putnam House: 85